The Living Pond

The Living Pond

Water Gardens with Fish
& Other Creatures

Helen Nash

Sterling Publishing Co., Inc.
New York

As always, a special thank you to my dear friend and editor Hannah Reich. This book would not have been possible were it not for the generous sharing of information, talent, and garden visions of many: Beau Roye, Betty Bissonnette, Bill Fintel, Bill Hawk, Bob BonGiorno, Charles A. Henne, Charles Phelps, Chuck and Shirley Rush, Darlene Jennings, Dick Weidener, Donna Howard, Dr. Erik Johnson, Eamonn Hughes, Frank and Annie Mikel, Gary Cryer, George Davis, James and Dee Murphy, Jim Kennedy, Joe Van Hook, Joe Zuritsky, Kit Knotts, Paula Biles, Perry D. Slocum, Phil Hunter, Renee Sullivan, Richard Norcross, Ron and Mary Ann Bergman, Ron Everhart, Steve Childers, Steve Kinney, Steve Stroupe, Vivian McCord, Wally and Nancy Oyler, and "Wink" Winkemier.

Library of Congress Cataloging-in-Publication Data

Nash, Helen, 1944-
  The living pond : water gardens with fish & other creatures / Helen Nash.
    p. cm.
  ISBN 0-8069-0705-3
  1. Water gardens. 2. Fish ponds. 3. Aquatic animals. I. Title.
  SB423.N364 2000
  635.9'674—dc21

                                                    00-041319

              1 3 5 7 9 10 8 6 4 2

           Uncredited photography is by the author

     Design and layout by Carol Malcolm Russo/Signet M Design, Inc.

             First paperback edition published in 2002 by
                    Sterling Publishing Company, Inc.
              387 Park Avenue South, New York, N.Y. 10016
                          © 2000 by Helen Nash
                   Distributed in Canada by Sterling Publishing
             ℅ Canadian Manda Group, One Atlantic Avenue, Suite 105
                       Toronto, Ontario, Canada M6K 3E7
               Distributed in Great Britain and Europe by Cassell PLC
            Wellington House, 125 Strand, London WC2R 0BB, England
             Distributed in Australia by Capricorn Link (Australia) Pty. Ltd.
                    P.O. Box 704, Windsor, NSW 2756 Australia

              Sterling ISBN 0-8069-0705-3 Hardcover
                        0-8069-7681-0 Paperback

In appreciation of three dear souls
who so willingly share their knowledge
and love of the life within our backyard waters:

Dr. Erik Johnson,
Bob BonGiorno,
and Bill Fintel.

Contents

Introduction

Water gardening and fish ponds have become accessible to everyone. Their primary attractions are the peace and tranquility they add to the life of our backyards. Because it is so easy to enhance our lives with a small pond, we often don't become aware of the true magic of water in the garden until the deed is done. There is life in the water…and lives around it that share in its attraction!

Usually we plan for the life in the water — plants and, of course, fish — goldfish, koi, and even native fish. But the pond's life is more encompassing than that. Frogs, toads, turtles, and newts delight in our pond habitats. Dragonflies, butterflies, and birds discover the water from the air. As we realize our ponds provide sanctuary for all these lives, we seek to maximize the close interrelationship of our gardens and the lives they attract. Whether we enhance an existing water feature or create one, we can tailor our constructions to best serve specific life.

Too often, we who are captivated by the idea of a pond in the garden dig the hole, line it, and then trek to the pet store to announce, "I have a pond, and I need some fish." The fish we bring home may or may not be suited to the pond we have constructed. Several small koi swim happily…until we suddenly realize those cute little fish are growing too large for the pond. We visit a bait shop and return home with interesting crayfish that voraciously gobble our plants. An adorable, quarter-sized turtle who peeks from under a lily pad begins nibbling on that pad…and later, after he has grown larger, takes bites out of our fish.

Many of the lives we purposefully place within our ponds are very forgiving, at least initially. You may talk with pondkeepers who proudly announce they've kept koi or turtles or whatever for "years" and never paid any attention to water quality or environmental conditions. They may even declare they don't even feed their aquatic pets or ever clean their ponds. From our own experience, we can assure you that such careless keeping of aquatic pets is destined for disaster. Wastes accumulate and bio-loads increase, eventually maxing out. Science is science. Eventually, the water

will begin to smell...and your pets will sicken and die. It can happen overnight, unexpectedly and suddenly, after years of carefree, successful pondkeeping.

If we haven't planned our water feature to satisfy the needs of the lives that inhabit it, we risk the loss or disappearance of those lives. That turtle or little green frog quickly seeks other water if no food remains, and fish too large for a small pond or too many in number languish and die. To best enjoy our backyard ponds and the lives they nourish, we need to plan our features to accommodate their needs. Whether you are planning your first or your tenth pond, consider which "pets" will call it home. Design and build your feature to allow yourself to tend healthy and happy lives. While there are many ways to build a pond for any one type of pet, certain basic guidelines should be met to ensure success. Once you've built the habitat, arm yourself with enough information about your pets to keep them in good health. The information in this book should help your efforts.

Enjoy the lives within and around your pond!

Helen Nash

CHAPTER ONE

Fish for Your Pond

Fish add life to the garden pond.

Even if your pond is for growing aquatic plants like water lilies, you'll want to include fish to control mosquitos. Because fish offer fascination and satisfaction in their own right, they may be part of your basic pond plan, or they may be your primary objective. For the healthiest fish, you'll want to select breeds that either suit your existing pond, or you'll want to design and build your pond to suit your selected species.

Types of Fish for Garden Ponds

Goldfish

The goldfish is the most commonly kept fish in the garden pond. Inexpensive goldfish are readily available in pet stores and are sold in bait shops as "feeder" goldfish. Often the goldfish carried by pet stores are raised as feeders too. Hatcheries breed feeder goldfish knowing that the fish will not live long lives. These fish are used as fishing bait or are stocked as food for larger, carnivorous fish such as bass. For that reason, many hatcheries do not take special precautions to

Fish help control mosquitos in the garden pond.

ensure the health of these fish. If you are purchasing feeder goldfish, check the fish and their tankmates carefully to be sure they are healthy specimens for your pond.

With the popularity of water gardening has come the breeding of goldfish specifically for garden ponds. Breeders of these fish take care to ensure the health of the fish. A wide selection of goldfish breeds may be kept in your pond—comets, black moors, fantails, shubunkins, and orandas. Goldfish with bubble caps and bubble eyes require greater care and may not be suited to outdoor ponds, particularly in colder climates or in ponds constructed with stones that might damage

their delicate bubbles. Goldfish breeds coexist happily with aquatic plants, and they require no more than 18 to 24 inches of water.

Plan to maintain the pond's stocking level at no more than one inch of fish per square foot of exposed water surface. This figure is based on maintaining a healthy chemical balance in the water and on providing adequate oxygen in the water to support the fish life. Even though aeration may be provided by a waterfall or a fountain, the primary oxygen exchange occurs at the water's surface. If you have significant surface coverage from plants, you should consider a lighter load of fish. As your fish load approaches the maximum stocking level, maintenance of the pond increases dramatically. You will need some sort of bio-filtration to handle the bio-load, the filter requiring regular care. You'll also want to test the water weekly to be sure that ammonia and nitrite, both harmful to fish, are not accumulating in the water. (See Chapter 4.)

When the weather warms in the spring, your goldfish will spawn or breed. This involves a vigorous chasing of females by males. Eggs are deposited among plants, and the needle-thin fry hatch a few days later. With plant cover in the pond and in the absence of frogs, you will find many baby fish populating your pond. While spawning usually occurs in the spring, a season of great temperature fluctuations results in spawnings as often as three weeks apart. Baby fish do count in your fish load. Friends with ponds or even a local pet store may be happy to adopt your excess fish. Your other option, of course, is to dig out another pond for your extra fish.

Goldfish are a sociable fish that coexist with other species of fish within the same pond. If you keep slower-moving species of goldfish, such as fantails, with faster and more mobile species, plan feeding regimens to accommodate each species. Remain with your fish during the feeding period, which is usually five to ten minutes once or twice a day. You can then monitor the slow swimmers to be sure they are fed. Unlike some other animals, fish feed only until sated. Presenting food for the slower fish after the more aggressive ones have finished tends to the needs of all.

Common Goldfish (Wakin)

Probably the hardiest of the breed, the common goldfish has short fins and a slender body. Young fish are a brownish blue-black that gradually fades away to yellow, orange, or white. A young fish purchased with

blackish marks, for example, is likely to lose all such markings within a year of purchase. Likewise, a red or orange and white fish may eventually turn all white. Environmental conditions, sunlight, and the fish's physical condition all affect the decoloring phase. Although white is considered an inferior fish, keeping at least one white fish in the pond serves as a barometer of water quality since the telltale fin and tail blushing that indicates stress is easily noticed. An active fish, the common goldfish outcompetes more delicate and slower-moving relatives such as fantails and orandas. The common goldfish grows to seven or eight inches at maturity.

Comet Goldfish

Developed in the United States, comets are one of the most popular and hardy fish for the garden pond. With a long, slender body and a long, flowing tail, these fish are red, orange, or red and white. A yellow strain has been developed in Great Britain. Both the red or the yellow may be all white with a circle of color on the top of the head, much like the tancho koi pattern. A very active fish, they outcompete slower-moving species for food. Comets measure six to ten inches at maturity.

Shubunkin

Another extremely hardy single-tailed goldfish, the shubunkin is a calico-colored species that may have either a short or a longer tail. Patches of blue coloring are overlaid with

Shubunkins are commonly called "calico" goldfish. Photo courtesy of Blue Ridge Fish Hatchery

blotches of red, orange, yellow, and brown, often with speckles of black all over the body. Shubunkins may not have the blue color present at all. They are quick swimmers that compete well for food. They measure six to ten inches at maturity. In selecting a young fish, avoid babies with very long flowing fins as they can develop health problems later when the fins actually grow too long for the body.

Fantail

Fantail goldfish are among the most elegant of pond fish. With long flowing fins and tails, they display the same range of colors found in common, comet, and shubunkin goldfish. Chinese-bred fantails tend to have a more pronounced and higher hump in their back. In all, their bodies are compressed, sometimes appearing to have a very full, sagging belly. Their body structure does not allow the rapid, darting movements seen in the more streamlined species. Generally hardy in a two-foot-deep pond in zones as cold as 4 and 5, they should be monitored for adequate feeding if faster fish are kept with them in the pond.

Oranda

The oranda looks like a fantail goldfish with a protruding, warty cap on its head. This growth is filled with air pockets that may be damaged by sharp or abrasive objects in the pond. Orandas may be kept outdoors in a pond, but pond owners in zones 4 and colder should winter them indoors in an aquarium, as their caps make them susceptible to problems in extremely cold temperatures. A deep enough pond in zone 5 allows them to remain outdoors year-round. The red-capped oranda is very popular; this fish is all white with a red cap. Orandas are available in all red, red and white, orange-yellow, silver-blue, and calico. The "bubble" hood does not begin developing until the fish is about six months old. Hoods develop best in algae-free water that is shaded from the harshest midday sun. Feeding tubifex worms or bloodworms (*Chironomus* larvae) to orandas promotes optimum cap growth. (These tiny, wriggly, red worms are often found in the filter of your pond where the water moves slowly enough to allow their midge parents to lay eggs.) A slow-moving fish, the oranda kept with faster fish must be monitored during feeding sessions.

Black Moor

Often described as a black, bug-eyed fish, the black moor was originally bred for Chinese nobility in the 1700s. Not all black moors develop the protruding eyes. While this is considered a flaw, such fish may prove better choices for the outdoor pond. Although young moors are black, at about two years of age the black begins to fade from the belly upward, so a mature black moor may end up a reddish or dull gold color. Choosing a fish of the deepest

A mature fantail with long, flowing fins also develops a very deep and shortened body that makes for a slow, waddling style of swimming.

black without any gold-tinted scales gives you a better chance of ending up with a mature black moor that stays black. With poorer vision and more sensitive eyes than other pond fish, black moors should be monitored during feeding sessions. Their sensitive eyes make them good candidates for winter aquariums in zones 5 and colder. At maturity, they measure five to six inches long.

Golden Orfe

Although illegal in some states in the U.S. because they are so prolific, golden orfe are a popular fish option for the water garden. A long, slender, golden yellow to peach-colored fish, often with brown spots on the head, these fish must be kept in quantity, as they are a schooling fish. If you keep only one or two orfe in your pond, they will languish and die.

A most rapid swimmer, the orfe is usually seen darting close to the surface of the pond. For that reason, many newcomers to water gardening think that orfe are needed to control insects. *All fish will eat insects on the surface of your pond water*. You should plan to include orfe in your pond only if you have a large enough pond to accommodate an active, schooling fish that matures at 18 inches or longer. In a large enough pond, orfe will winter over in zones 4 and 5 and warmer. Orfe tend to be more sensitive to water quality and chemicals than goldfish; successful orfe-keeping requires close attention to pond chemistry.

Koi

In Japan, where breeding koi has become an art, these magnificent fish are family pets and respected good luck charms. They are the domesticated, colored form of the wild common carp, *Cyprinus carpio*. Although the young koi you see at a pet

The great variety of colors and patterns available in Koi explains why the large breed is known as the "jewel of the pond." Photo of the Weideners' Koi pond in Louisville, Kentucky

Stocking too many Koi in a garden pond results in poor water quality, both visually, in particulate wastes and green water, and chemically.

koi, besides their size, is their limitless range of color. Specific color patterns are defined by Japanese names. Showing koi is a grand hobby, with show-quality koi fetching enviable sums of money, but lovely koi are available to the hobbyist at reasonable prices. One of the most enjoyable aspects of keeping koi is watching their colors develop as the fish mature. It is said that every koi show has a winner that began as a bargain from a chain or a pet store.

Because of their greater size, koi have very different needs from goldfish. While goldfish may be kept in a shallow water garden, koi need at least three feet of depth. The ideal backyard koi pond is four to five feet deep, with koi ponds in the coldest climates being another two feet deeper. Most pond experts recognize the difference between koi keeping and goldfish-keeping by recommending that you maximally stock *one-half inch of koi per square foot of the pond's exposed surface area*, as compared with the one-inch per square foot suggested for goldfish.

A pondkeeper addicted to koi, however, has a difficult time keeping his/her fish load below such maximum stocking levels. There is always another color pattern that must be included. Since koi are best kept in water of good quality,

store are comparable in size to goldfish, koi *are not goldfish.* Physically, even the smallest of koi display the characteristic double pair of barbels at the mouth that are not found in goldfish. In only two or three years, a small koi can grow to be 24 inches long. A mature koi may be three feet long and weigh over 22 pounds (10kg).

The primary attraction of

koi ponds usually make use of bio-filters that allow maximum stocking of the pond.

You might compare the pond behavior of koi to that of a herd of cattle in a field — grazing all day long. Actually, no fish has a stomach that is filled by three square meals a day; they all nibble throughout the day. Small goldfish nibble on the mossy algae growing on your pond walls, as well as on tender, submerged grasses. Because koi grow to such size, however, their constant grazing wreaks havoc in the planted water garden. Only the most lushly planted water garden can survive the onslaught of a herd of mature, grazing koi.

Since koi consider your pond plants their own smorgasbord, and because most water gardens are in the two-foot-depth range to accommodate the plants, the typical water garden is not the best home for koi. Many koi keepers use salt in the pond water as a tonic for their koi. Although some aquatic plants tolerate brackish water, most—especially water lilies and submerged grasses—suffer in salted water. Tending to the health of your koi may set you at odds with the health of your aquatic plants.

Yet another way that koi wreak havoc in the water garden is the fishy habit of nosing about in substrata, especially the gravel topping of your

Some long-finned or butterfly Koi feature fluffy "eyebrows" that provide further interest to this new breed of pond fish.

aquatic plants, in search of delectable insect larvae. A two-foot-long koi bears a good-sized nose for rooting around your plants; it is not uncommon for koi to fully unearth your plants. If you want both koi and aquatic plants, consider some of the variations shown in Chapter 3 on koi ponds.

Butterfly Koi

In the 1980s a new breed of koi became available: the butterfly koi. These koi display wonderfully long, flowing fins and tails. In recent years breeders have developed many color variations, too. Although the hype was that these were a smaller version of koi and that they could be kept in smaller ponds than those recommended for koi, mature butterfly koi are every bit as large as their short-finned koi relatives. Likewise, their behavior is the same as their counterparts. Consider their habitat needs the same as for koi.

Gambuzia, White Clouds, and Rosy Red Minnows

These fish are excellent selections for the smaller pond or tub garden. None grow to more than two inches long. However, they are best in the warm-climate pond. None can be reliably wintered year after year in zone 5 or colder; they must be wintered indoors in aquariums or in setups that have room-temperature water. They are especially well suited to the tropical pond. Prolific breeders, their numbers require control to avoid upsetting the balance of water chemistry.

Native Fish

The question always arises: Can I keep native fish in my backyard pond? Besides the matter of size of the pond, the really critical issue in trying to keep native fish in a backyard

pond is water temperature. Most native fish found in our lakes and rivers are cold-water fish. They will not survive in shallow bodies of water that quickly heat to 75°F or more in the summer. Winter temperatures present another problem in that backyard ponds usually lack the necessary depth for a proper thermal layer for hibernation. In our own backyard pond, we raised some blue gill that were introduced by a charitable mallard duck. They did fine for two years, as the winters were mild. They multiplied in great numbers; however, during the first harsh winter, fewer than ten survived. All goldfish and koi lived.

Catfish, particularly the albino species, are a native fish often considered for the backyard pond. Known as "bottom feeders" and "scavengers," these fish are often thought of by new pond owners as fish that help keep the pond clean. In reality, they keep the normal sediment collecting on the pond bottom stirred up, making the water murky. As catfish attain mature growth, often around 20 inches long, they become bullies about food. Their wide mouths become vacuum cleaners, sucking in all floating food, even as they bump away the koi and goldfish you seek also to feed. Injury to your domesticated fish is not uncommon. Consider, also, that those wide

mouths can engulf a good-sized goldfish.

Fish such as trout require a fresh flow of water through their habitat. Predatory fish such as bass require a constantly replenished supply of smaller, feeder fish. Keeping native fish often involves setting up a food chain within your pond that must be carefully orchestrated. To determine if keeping native fish in your pond is desirable or possible, contact your state's department of natural resources or your local county extension agent for regulations and information. State and private fish hatcheries are another source of information. Generally, keeping native fish involves planning an earth-bottom pond of some size and appropriate depth.

Purchasing Fish for Your Pond

Bringing home sick or infected fish endangers the existing pool inhabitants and creates a sad, stressful, and expensive situation as fish become ill, are treated, and perhaps die. Purchase fish only from a reputable dealer. (If no dealer is near you, consider some of the many reputable mail-order houses. Fish are shipped safely all over the world.)

Carefully observe the fish in the tank from which you will purchase your pond fish. Frayed or split fins, white spots, or wounds indicate serious health problems that may be contagious or terminal.

Often you will bring new fish home in a plastic bag.

Talk to the vendor. Does the seller know the basics of common fish diseases and infestations? Can the vendor describe symptoms of these problems? Does the vendor regularly employ preventive treatments of health problems?

Observe the fish. Clamped fins, ragged fins or tail, and abnormal blotching or marking may indicate health problems. Other common signs of problems include fish hovering in a corner or at the bottom of the aquarium tank, fish being nudged by other fish in the tank, or fish being easily caught (little fear of being handled). A healthy fish is active and sociable with its kind.

Carefully observe other fish in the tank. Many diseases and infestations are contagious. If another fish in the tank appears ill, do not buy any fish from the tank. Avoid purchasing fish from tanks that appear to be self-contained but are in fact sharing the same recycled water with many other tanks.

Avoid purchasing fish that have recently arrived at the store. Allow time for transportation shock to disappear so you can be sure behavior aberrations are not due to disease. This also allows time for the shop to provide preventive treatment for parasites. Even though the fish might initially seem healthy, the stress of transportation may make it susceptible to free-swimming parasites or bacteria in the water. Such infestations may not appear for 10 to 14 days at pet shop aquarium temperatures.

Be especially cautious if the pet shop guarantees their fish for shorter periods of time than a parasite's life cycle. Most reputable shops quarantine new fish for two or three weeks before offering them for sale.

Transporting Fish

Fish are usually transported from the pet store to your pond with the fish enclosed in a plastic bag partially filled with water and then inflated with pure oxygen. If the fish are to be transported some distance, advise the proprietor so that extra care may be taken. In any event, the fish should be handled as little as possible to avoid disturbing its protective slime coating. Some dealers use a stress coat additive that may offer slime coat protection; however, this can also disrupt gill function. A salt tonic dose added to the water stimulates slime coat production and relieves stress.

Transporting fish in a bucket of water may require a battery-operated air pump for lengthy trips. Without such aeration, hand-splash the water every half hour of the trip. Keep the bucket covered to prevent the fish from jumping out!

Keep the fish as shaded and cool as possible. Professional fish shippers place the bagged fish in a closed Styrofoam box with a frozen pack beneath the bag. Keeping the water chilled during long trips slows the fish's metabolism, awareness, and need for oxygen.

Most pond fish are poikilothermic—they do not maintain a constant body temperature as do warm-blooded animals. The fish's body temperature varies according to the temperature of the water. Fish can adjust to gradual changes in water temperature, but sudden changes of even two degrees can stress the fish. A 10-degree difference in water temperature can kill the fish. For this reason, we float the plastic bag containing the fish in the water the fish will be released into. After 10 to 15 minutes of such floating, you can add some pond water to the bag and continue floating it until the temperatures have equalized. If this operation is performed in direct sunlight, drape a towel over the bag to protect the fish.

Do not add the water the fish is transported in to your pond or quarantine tank since it may harbor the free-swimming stage of parasites. Once the water in the floating bag has equalized with the pond water, transfer the fish by hand. Large fish should be guided by net into shallow containers of pond water. If the fish are being placed directly into your pond, dip the fish for 10 to 15 seconds in a salt dip of one pound of non-iodized salt per gallon of water.

Fish transported in a bucket are kept covered with a towel or screen to protect them from sunlight as well as to prevent them from jumping out. Add pond water to the bucket a few cupfuls at a time, removing the same amount of water from the bucket, slowly providing time for the temperature adjustment.

For the sake of the fish already in your pond, new fish should be quarantined for two weeks in a hospital tank that has one to two tablespoons of non-iodized salt per five gallons of water dissolved in it. A broad-spectrum parasiticide may be used as well. If a quarantine is not possible, the entire pool may be treated with a broad-spectrum parasiticide or a one percent salt dose every three days for three treatments.

Remember that a fish's health is directly related to its environment. For example, you'll want to avoid transporting fish when the water temperature is above 90°F, since fish are less able to manage stress at high temperatures. *Any* change can produce stress, which can cause the fish to slough off its protective slime coating. The immune system of the fish is in the slime coating; without it the fish is susceptible to disease, infection, or parasites that normally may be present in the water. Snails, for example, may

Your garden pond creates a cherished sense of peace and tranquility. Including fish is an important part of its creation.

be the intermediary host for anchor worm. If you have snails in your pond, be very careful not to stress your new fish when they are introduced into the pond.

Signs of stress in fish are frantic jumping and swimming, hiding, clamped fins, blushing fins, and red body veining. Commercial Stress Coat products help prevent the loss of cellular fluids and electrolytes and provide a coating that may prevent abrasions, but they cannot replace the enzymes within the slime coat that fight parasites and disease. The general dosage is one teaspoon per 10 to 20 gallons of water. This treatment can be added to the transport bag, the quarantine tank, or the pond. A highly stressed fish should not be treated with such products as they may impair the gill functions.

Salt at a rate of 2.5 g/l or 2 pounds per 100 gallons acts as both a stress reliever and a general tonic. Salt stimulates the fish to produce its own slime coating. In treating the entire pond, compute the volume in gallons and then divide by 100. Multiply this figure by two pounds to determine the dosage to be used in each of two treatments at a three-day interval. *Remove all plants from the pond before treatment.* Dissolve the salt in a bucket of pond water and distribute it around the edge in the water.

Whether your new fish are placed directly in the pond or in a quarantine tank, keep a close eye on them for the first few hours to be certain they are adjusting to their new quarters. A screen or a net over the tank or pond will prevent any from jumping out. Don't be deceived by an apparently calm reaction initially. It may take an hour or so before the fish adjusts enough to begin moving about. Keep their quarters covered for the first couple days when you are not present. Likewise, feed sparingly the first few days to allow transport recovery.

Even if you purchase inexpensive fish for your pond, they become treasured family pets. For that reason alone, select breeds that can exist healthily in your existing pond, or construct a pond to suit the breeds you plan to keep. Successful fish keeping goes beyond mere pond construction; it also involves maintaining the pond. Unlike large bodies of water existing naturally in the wild, a pond is a closed system—an outdoor aquarium—for your backyard fish. A basic knowledge of water chemistry and fish health makes for success.

If you ask people why they install a pond or water feature in their gardens, the answer is almost unanimous: "For the peace and tranquility." Peace and tranquility are assured beyond the mere aesthetics of water in the garden when your creation exists in harmony with itself and with the world beyond. Planning assures your living pond will be a life-giving source of peace and tranquility for you and for the Earth.

CHAPTER TWO

The Goldfish Pond

The water garden is a perfect home for goldfish.

*W*ith the popularity of water gardening have come several myths and sales pitches. You might hear that putting in a water garden does not put you in the business of filtering water. Yet the moment you introduce fish into that pond, you are in the water-quality business. Even the least expensive feeder goldfish acquires a name and becomes a family pet. That pet deserves your responsible attention. Your fish need oxygenated water and water free of toxic chemicals such as ammonia, nitrite, and hydrogen sulfide. To accommodate those needs, you may need to be concerned with filtration—be it mechanical, vegetative, or biological. Even the way you design and build the pond impacts critical issues of water quality.

Designing the Goldfish Pond

A goldfish pond is basically a water garden—a pond used for growing aquatic plants. Unless you live in more extreme climate zones, such as the colder 3 and 4 or the hotter 9 and 10, this pond need be no deeper

Goldfish add extra life and color to the garden pond.

than two feet, the typical depth of an aquatic plant pond. In extreme climates, providing a deeper portion of three feet allows for respite during the heat of summer and/or the cold of winter.

The usual considerations of designing a water garden for plants come into play: site the pond where you can most enjoy it. Assuming that you will include water lilies, you want the pond to enjoy at least three hours of direct sunlight each day. Shady sites can be chosen, but your planting options will be limited.

Do you need to include shallow (6- to 12-inch-deep) planting shelves around the perimeter of your pond? With two schools of thought on this, you must decide which design

best fits your needs and situation. Planting shelves provide shallow areas for emergent marginal aquatic plants, such as pickerel (*Pontederia*), arrowhead (*Sagittaria*), or sweet flag (*Acorus*). They also offer a safety area, if the shelf is wide enough, for children's accidental tumbles into the pond, as well as "steps" for easy entry into and exit from the pond. However, shelves also offer predators—particularly raccoons and herons—easy access to your pond. To protect both fish and plants, you may opt instead for planting pedestals of brick or block, or you may choose specially constructed plant stands so the sides of your pond can be nearly straight to the bottom.

To Filter or Not to Filter?

Do you need to include filtration plans in your pond design? We have many ponds of various sizes and construction, all without filtration or even recycling water of any kind. None of these ponds, save the large one lined with pea gravel that crashed after 10 years, has ever had a problem with green water or water chemistry. The most common cause of water-quality and water-clarity problems—too many fish—has never been a consideration in our ponds. We have too many frogs! The frogs are so diligent at eating small and baby fish, we have not seen baby fish in over 10 years. Our fish population has remained well below the problem level of supplying too much nutrient in the pond water that feeds algae and fish-threatening levels of ammonia and nitrite.

You need biofiltration when the fish load reaches its maximum level for the pond. The general formula is one inch of goldfish per square foot of exposed water surface. This formula is based on the water surface's being the primary oxygen source for your pond water. To determine the surface area of your pond, multiply the length by the width, in feet.

The fish load in your pond will change each year as the fish grow and multiply. *When their size and number approach the maximum level for your pond, you will need bio-filtration to help convert the ammonia wastes into relatively harmless nitrate.* Retrofitting a pond with a bio-filter is easily accomplished, or you can plan ahead to include it. Often vegetable filtration supplied by a planted stream or a smaller, shallow plant pond through which the water flows offers both nutrient removal to prevent green water and stone media for bacterial colonies that impact water chemistry. If your fish load is near the pond's maximum stocking level, you should test your water regularly to monitor ammonia and nitrite levels, regardless of what filtration, if any, you use. (See Chapter 4.)

Building a Goldfish Pond

Your goldfish pond can be a rigid, preformed pond. These ponds are typically small and seriously limit the number of fish that can be safely kept. Remember the formula: one inch of goldfish per square foot of exposed water surface. While preformed ponds offer ease of installation, consider your climate zone and its extremes of

When your fish population reaches the maximum stocking level for your pond, filtration is necessary to maintain clear and safe water.

heat and cold. If the preformed pond is only 18 inches deep and is installed in full sunlight, you will have to keep the water from overheating in hot weather as well as protect the fish from freezing in extreme cold.

Edging options for preformed ponds are limited. A small waterfall can be constructed with preformed units or built into a mound of dirt that is lined with rubber pond liner to prevent water loss. If you mound soil for a waterfall design, keep your mound within a pleasing relation to the size of the pond for the most natural appearance.

Using a flexible membrane such as synthetic rubber (EPDM) offers more latitude in size and design of the pond. Recycling water requires the use of a pump and electricity. You'll want your pond installed near a safe, grounded electrical source, as well as near a water source to top off or maintain the pond.

Selecting a site that naturally collects standing water may seem obvious, but that location invites runoff to drain into the pond, and such water sometimes contains dangerous lawn chemicals. Groundwater may also push your pond construction up from the ground. Check your water table before digging the pond hole—if groundwater may present a problem, you'll want to install a French drain to channel the water elsewhere and to preserve the integrity of your pond. *If you must install a drainage system, be sure to dig it to a depth slightly deeper than the deepest portion of your pond.* The trench housing the perforated drain should deepen an inch per every ten linear feet to its final drainage point.

Small preformed ponds make for easy installation of a water feature.

As a result of a high water table, this pond liner has been pushed out of the excavation.

Installing a French drain to take groundwater away from the pond site prevents future problems. Photo by Oliver Jackson

Although a preformed pond is the quickest way to start ponding, most pond owners voice one regret about their first pond: too small! Larger ponds are possible with synthetic liners such as EPDM (ethylene propylene diene monmer). A 45-mil-thick liner is more than adequate for a pond. EPDM is available in a thicker 60 mil. This is less flexible but perhaps more suited to the pond owner who also keeps large water-loving dogs. Generally, avoid creating coves and complicated designs that encourage stagnant areas in the pond. Such designs also require unsightly folding of the liner. Folds are also conducive to hidden sediment collection, encouraging the growth of anaerobic bacteria, which produce fish-toxic hydrogen sulfide.

Consider Pond Maintenance

Pond maintenance is a major consideration in your design plans. You may think that the black liner of your pond looks artificial and that lining the bottom with loose rocks or gravel will make it look more natural. In time, however, mosslike algae will coat and camouflage the liner. Your goldfish and plants will also produce particulate organic wastes on the pond bottom. As they build up, anaerobic conditions will invite the bacteria that use these wastes as food. A by-product of this consumption is fish-toxic hydrogen sulfide. This is the reason pond owners are often advised to keep a hole open in the ice during the winter. The hole allows gas exchange and the escape of toxic gases.

Sediment buildup can be controlled with regular pond cleaning—using a pond vac as part of your regular water exchange, using a swimming-pool skimmer net to scoop it up, or using a shop vac during annual cleaning, for example. Borrowing from the koi-keeping hobby, installing a bottom drain may ease maintenance and help to create safe water conditions. Adding loose rocks or gravel to the bottom of the pond can create more problems than it is worth as the organic sediment filters down among the rocks, treacherously unseen.

Don't be fooled by the argu-

Trying to clean the bottom of a pond covered with rocks may be more work than you are willing to expend.

ment that you are duplicating conditions found in nature. As much as you would like to think you are recreating nature with your small pond in the back-yard, the fact remains that you are creating a closed system. In nature, healthy water systems have natural ways of flooding and replenishing. The fish inhabiting these systems have much more space in which to exist than is offered by your small duplication of nature. The ratio of wastes to water volume is not comparable. Think of your pond as an outdoor aquarium—a closed system that you make *appear* natural. Natu-ralize it with edging treatment and the surrounding land-scaping, not with its interior construction. Use rock linings in your stream construction, where flowing water encour-ages the growth of aerobic bac-teria that contribute to the health of your water. Plant flowing-water-loving/tolerant plants (watercress, water celery, dwarf sweetflag, or water irises) within the stream bed to help consume the col-lecting nutrients.

The sparkling, clear water found in nature exists in an open system of water replenish-ment and ecological interaction. Even planting directly into the gravel bottom of a small back-yard water garden does not duplicate the conditions found in nature. The most commonly

In nature, clear, sparkling water is considered an "open system," with natural ways of being cleaned and refreshed.

submerged aquatic so used is anacharis, or *Elodea canadensis*, a plant commonly described as a seaweed. Yes, these plants will grow roots and anchor them-selves in a substrate base in the pond. However, those plants derive most of their nutrients *directly from the water*, not through their roots in the substrate.

Relying on the bacteria *Bacillus subtilis*, commonly called a sludge eater, to rid the pond of dangerous accumula-tions of decomposing organic settlement works best when the settled material is exposed to fresh, oxygen-holding water. Sludge-eating bacteria are aer-obic. They cannot work deep down in accumulations between

layers of rock and gravel. They work on the surface of the buildup, gradually working their way down through it. A heavy sediment buildup takes time to work through. In the pond constructed without rocks or gravel on the bottom, this bacteria can be effective since more surface area of the sedi-ment is exposed to oxygenated water.

Cleaning a rock lining can be a real maintenance night-mare. Yes, you can remove the gravel, hose it off, and clean up the pond bottom. You may decide this work is worth the aesthetics. However, cleaning a large pond may be all but impossible. A pond vac may not be powerful enough to pull up the sediment. Providing a sump hole in the deepest point of the pond for a high-pressure hose to wash the sediment into presents two problems: 1. The rocks themselves present a maze that can trap too much of the sediment. 2. The submersible pump used in water gardens is not meant to pump sediment. A submersible water garden pump can easily burn up in pumping sediment; that's why mechanical filters are provided to prevent sediment from circulating through the pump. The obvious solution to this problem is to use a shop vac once the pond has been drained to the sump area. However, you still have the problem of ensuring that the sediment is making it to the sump!

If you consider a pond design with rocks or gravel on the pond bottom, realistically determine if you are willing to perform the maintenance. If you should find yourself too busy, the pond will crash. "Crashing" means that one morning you awaken to find all your fish floating belly up. If you named your fish, this is a major trauma. Our first pond was 80' × 50', and we lined it with pea gravel, naively thinking the gravel would hold down a liner installed over a slow-seeping spring. (And it looked so natural!) It took 10 years, but the pond crashed. Smaller ponds will crash in

Mortaring in the rocks on your pond liner keeps from creating dangerous sediment-collecting pockets. Photo by Eamonn Hughes

three to five years. A good indication that your pond is heading in this direction is what your nose tells you. A healthy water garden or fish pond does not give off a bad odor. Ponds that smell rank, particularly with the odor of rotten eggs, are into a downward spiral and without a serious cleaning will crash.

The Best Way to Camouflage Your Pond Liner

There is, however, a way to line the bottom of your pond with natural-looking stone: mortar the cobbles into place. The spaces between the stones are then filled with mortar that prevents organic matter from accumulating beyond the reach

of your cleaning efforts or the work of *Bacillus subtilis*. Yes, this takes longer to construct, but when you consider that your pond will last for many years, taking an extra week to construct it is negligible. The only precaution to take with this construction method is to fill, drain, refill, and redrain several times until the water pH reading indicates that the lime in the mortar is no longer impacting the water chemistry and posing a threat to the fish you will keep. (See Chapter 4.)

Installing a Preformed Pond

Before beginning excavation, set the preformed pond in its future location and check the ground levels for the entire site.

Preformed

Pond

Installations

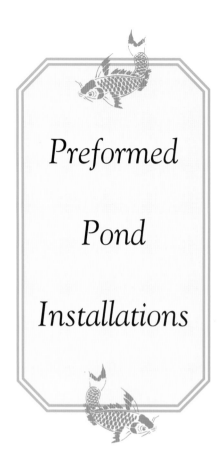

Build a camouflaging box around the above-ground preformed pond. Be sure to provide concrete blocks to the pond wall to prevent collapse.

Construct a free-form deck to hide the edges of the preformed pond.

Use landscaping blocks to hide the edge of the larger preformed pond.

Insert the preformed pond within the edge of a boardwalk, and edge the pond with rocks.

Set the preformed ponds within a raised planting bed.

Mark the levels on stakes before digging. You may have to use some of your excavated soil to build up areas to achieve a level pond edge. Water does rest level within its bed, oblivious to the top edge of that site. By keeping the upper pond edge fully level all around, you avoid a lopsided appearance. Remember to tamp firmly any soil that is used in altering elevation to avoid settling later that will throw off your level.

If your preformed pond is symmetrical, you can turn it upside down to mark its outline on the site with chalk, spray paint, or kitty litter. Otherwise, set the form on the site and use a weighted string hung over the upper edge to mark your excavation guidelines.

Excavate a shovel's depth at a time across the entire outlined form. Compare the depth of any planting shelves with the shovel depth. Excavate the entire form to this depth. Set the pond shell back on the site and mark around the pond's lowest level.

Once the excavation is completed, use a carpenter's level to verify the perfect levels of the shelves and bottom. This is important since the shell will rest upon the highest point of ground, unlike a flexible membrane that will conform to the excavation. While you may have established a level upper edge, not attending to shelf and bottom levels can negate your

Flexible liner membranes allow you to create large, free-form pond designs.

efforts. Clear away any loose soil, rocks, and roots. Smooth a two-inch sand cushion over the entire bottom and shelves, tamping and carefully checking that the levels are maintained. Keep a hose handy to spray the sand as necessary. Dry sand slides easily from a shelf and disrupts your levels by accumu-

The Living Pond

lating on the next lower cut. This sand cushion acts as a buffer against ground heaving where the ground might freeze and prevents the pond form from cracking or being forced out of kilter.

Set the pond into its excavation and check the level of the top edges as you fill the pond with an inch or two of water. While the water is still low in the filling pond, grasp the pond edge and jiggle it to correct minor leveling discrepancies. As the pond fills, use a slowly running hose to wash or flush sand gently into the excavation. Washing in the side-fill helps prevent air pockets that cause uneven settling of the surrounding ground. Fill the pond nearly full, simultaneously washing sand down the sides of the excavation so backfilling and water filling take place at about the same rate. Continue to monitor the level of the top edge of the pond. Once the pond is fully installed and is level, complete the edging.

Another installation option with a preformed pond shell is to set it on the ground and build an attractive wall around it. Be sure the chosen site is fully level. Whether you camouflage the outer walls with stonework or set your pond within a raised planting bed, you must provide support for the walls of the form or they will buckle and crack. Water is heavy and its

pressure easily buckles the walls of an unsupported pond form.

Installing a Lined Pond

A watertight membrane offers the most design flexibility for your goldfish/water-garden pond. The least expensive materials, such as thin plastics or swimming-pool liners, are not recommended. Even heavier grades of plastic sheeting puncture easily and degrade quickly, often in less than three years. Vinyl swimming-pool liners may be treated with algicides that prove toxic over time to fish and plants. Their light color may also appear too artificial and may be difficult to naturalize within the garden setting.

PVC liners are more durable and can be expected to last 10 to 15 years. They do, however, require protection from sunlight to prevent UV degradation. Sunlight can make plastics brittle. They will crack and split open. If you select a form of PVC, be sure to install edging that overhangs the edge enough that the liner is not exposed to sunlight at all. The liner below the water level is safe.

Probably the most popular liner today is the synthetic rubber EPDM (ethylene propylene diene monmer). Sold in weights of 45-mil and 60-mil, it is resis-

tant to UV degradation and offers a 50-year life expectancy. The 60-mil is more difficult to work with than the 45-mil; its folds are cumbersome. Fortunately, the 45-mil is quite adequate for most pond constructions.

Always use some form of protection or underlay between a flexible liner and the pond excavation. Rocks work their way up through the soil; underlay helps protect the liner from sharp edges that may surface in time. While you may use a thick layer of newspaper (spray lightly with water as you work to prevent it from blowing about) or scraps of carpeting (slash the underside to prevent it from pocketing water and floating up your liner), the easiest option is a geothermal textile that allows water to flow through as it obstructs objects and soil. This textile is commonly called "underlay fabric."

Although the size may be calculated and the liner purchased before the excavation, it is best to wait until the excavation is completed and final measurements can be taken. This allows you to accommodate last-minute changes necessitated by hidden debris, abandoned septic systems, or large rocks. Unless any sidewalls, including shelves, are only gently sloped, the shelves should be added to the computation. The base figures come from the maximum width and length of the pond, regardless of shape. Add to each figure any depths from top to shelf, shelf to bottom, or top to bottom, as required. If the entire pond has a planting shelf, the depths from the top to the shelf and the shelf to the pond bottom may be doubled to account for the same measurements on the opposite side. The depth figures must account for the depths on opposite sides of the pond and must be added to *both* the width and length base figures. At least an extra foot should be added to the width and length figures to allow for an extra six inches around the upper edge that will come up behind the pond edging.

Liner Size: Maximum Length + 2 Depths + 1 Foot × Maximum Width + 2 Depths + 1 Foot

As with any other type of pond installation, the levels should be established before any excavation is begun. With a lined pond, the shelves and pond bottom need not be perfectly level; it is the *upper* edge of the pond that determines that the water level will appear the same on all sides of the pond.

Soil type permitting, the sides of the pond should be excavated as steeply as possible. This allows the top edging to best conceal the liner. Vertical

sides coming down from plant shelves make it easy to step out of the pond. A sloped side is slippery and dangerous to walk on. Naturally, clay soils are the easiest to carve shelves and pond sides in. Should the soil be sandy or loamy, make the slope more gradual. Especially in sandy soils, you may have to use plywood to form and rein-

A carpenter's bubble level, available in several sizes, helps you determine that your excavation is level from side to side and around the perimeter. Photo courtesy of Maryland Aquatic Nurseries

force the construction shell. Concrete building blocks also work well. Except in the heaviest clay, expect earth excavation to deteriorate over time. Planting shelves may lose their sharp edge and soil will

crumble to the next lower level, eventually creating a slope instead of defined levels. Especially if you will use heavy stonework around the pond edge, plan ahead for the settling and shifting ground.

Excavation proceeds with removing sod, marking the pond outline on the ground, and removing soil one shovelful deep at a time. Once the hole is deep enough to accommodate the planting shelf (if you will include one), mark the shelf to your desired width. If you plan to reinforce the walls with concrete blocks, include their thickness in your calculations. Remember that planting shelves provide access to the pond not only to you but also to predators such as herons and raccoons.

As you excavate to the bottom of the pond, slope the bottom to one deeper place for water drainage. This will make emptying and cleaning the pond easier. If you plan to install a bottom drain, this will be the site.

Clear the excavation of loose soil and any protruding roots or loose stones. Smooth a two-inch layer of sand over the bottom. Carefully fit an underlay over the entire excavation. If the underlay is cut from several pieces, anchor it with bricks or stone as you work.

While you work with the underlay, unfold the pond liner

Using loose rocks on the pond bottom complicates your pond maintenance and threatens your fish's health with hidden sediment and its resulting deadly toxin, hydrogen sulfide.

six inches overlaps fully around the upper perimeter. For the larger excavation, fold the liner in half and place it in the center of the hole. Unfold the liner, removing any weights on the underlay as you gradually ease the liner into the excavation. Fold the liner to fit your excavation as you work your way to the outer walls. Combine folds to create as few as possible. Corner folds mitered inward will appear smooth and flat from the outside.

Once the liner is folded and fitted, lightly anchor the excess at the top edges with stones or bricks. Assured the top edges of the excavation are fully level, begin adding water. Monitor the folds and adjust them as necessary as the water level rises. Fill the pond as near to the top as necessary to verify the level of the top edge and the settled fitting of the liner. Leave the pond alone for a day or two to allow any further settling. When you are ready to finish the top edge, use a submersible pump to remove enough water to allow comfortable workspace.

Even though the aging pond acquires a camouflage and natural appearance with a mossy algae coating (this is good!), you may wish to naturalize the pond bottom with cobbles or rocks. Remember that loose rocks create myriad pockets for organic sediment.

to warm in the sun. This eases any creases and fold marks. Wear gloves if the weather is warm; the black liner absorbs heat and may be surprisingly hot to the touch.

Drape the liner gently into the excavation so that at least

The Goldfish Pond

This is very hazardous for your fish and creates a maintenance nightmare for you. If you wish such an appearance, take the time to mortar the rocks into place over the pond liner. Mix your mortar in small portions and work a small area. The size and thickness of your rocks determines the thickness of the mortar in which they are set. You want the mortar to come up between the rocks so the sediment collecting between them can be removed easily in your pond cleaning. Note that a swimming pool skimmer net and an effective mechanical filter can control sediment buildup on a pond bottom free of stone. Cleaning a pond bottom fitted with mortared rocks will still require annually draining the pond. How you finish the pond bottom should depend, first of all, on providing the healthiest conditions for your fish. Second, consider the amount of time you can realistically dedicate to maintenance.

Installing a Waterfall/Stream

A waterfall may be a stacked arrangement of stair-stepping flat rocks, a channel of cobbled rocks, or an extended, higher stair-step construction. In any case, the courseway should be fully lined with flexible pond-liner membrane. The liner should extend—albeit hidden among rocks, soil, and plants—above the splash line of the channel to prevent water loss from the system. At the top of the system, perhaps tucked beneath the uppermost rocks or entering into a small pond/bio-filter setup, will be the end of the hosing that cycles water from the pond below.

Aesthetically, the waterfall/stream should be in a pleasing proportion to its reservoir pond. This may involve using soil from the pond excavation to create the higher ground through which your waterfall/stream will flow. Blending the higher ground into the existing terrain creates a pleasing effect. Practically, the water involved in the waterfall/stream system should not lower the reservoir pond's water level to any noticeable degree. In reservoir ponds with variously sized waterfall/stream constructions, you must consult a chart of water droppage. For the simple, stacked waterfall, this is of no concern. If you plan an extensive stream system that will be fed by the reservoir pond, this is a serious concern.

If you are using a flexible liner for your stream or waterfall courseway, the easiest construction is a separate piece of membrane. This piece should overlap the lower construction several inches. Throughout the courseway, separate pieces of

A waterfall is much like a stairway in construction, providing lowering levels to the pond's edge.

Each level section of a stream may be lined with a piece of liner that overlaps the next lower section.

liner may be used, always, however, overlapping a lower, lined elevation. Seaming pieces of liner that will rest underwater usually produces leaks in time.

As you build your waterfall, keep a hose handy to test the flow produced by your rock arrangement. Tilting the spillway rocks slightly forward ensures that the flow does not seep back into the construction. Use a carpenter's level to verify the level front edge of your rocks. This prevents the water from listing and flowing to one side of its channel. Be cautious that the distance from one level to the next is not so great that water is drawn back to the face of the structure, producing a "wet wall." Once you are satisfied with the arrangement, you may wish to mortar key structural rocks into place and perhaps backfill behind the front rocks with a poly spray that further prevents water loss. (Waterproof poly material is available in spray cans at hardware stores.)

In building either a waterfall or stream, excavate your channel deeply enough to accommodate the rocks you will use plus a two- to three-inch water depth along with enough edge height to prevent water loss. After covering the channel with an underlay and the liner material, begin your design with the larger side-framing rocks. Work your way across

the channel. Do not use mortar until you are fully satisfied with the final plan.

The wider the channel, the more dissipated and weaker will be your water flow. Generally, 100 gallons per hour of pump power is needed per inch of the width of the spillway. As you compute the size of the pump needed for your flow rate, remember to include the loss in flow for the pump to push the water to the top of a structure higher than one foot. Most pump charts include how many gallons per hour are pumped at various heights or lifts. For every ten feet of piping the water must flow through to the waterfall, add another foot of lift. Many people find the flow more pleasing with piping half an inch or an inch larger in diameter than the outlet provided on the pump. An adapter—either PVC, stainless steel, or bronze—is used between the pump and the piping. (Aluminum oxidizes and corrodes in pond water.) The piping may be rigid, potable white PVC or flexible black PVC.

A stream construction presents specific considerations. Since the water flows through it allowing oxygenated water to help cleanse the system, you can use rocks or gravel to create a natural appearance in its bed. However, you will want to make sure that the media you

select is not moved along with the water. A sandy-bottom stream may suit you aesthetically, but flowing water is likely to carry it to the first obstruction, where it will dam up the courseway. Loose rocks often present problems; water flows under rather than over them. You may decide to simply mortar small stones and cobbles onto the liner bed. As with the waterfall, begin with the outer wall construction and work your way across the channel.

While your stream design can be one long channel, you may opt for a sectioned construction in which a short waterfall or a cobbled section drops to the next level. So long

Both waterfall and stream constructions begin with large, framing rocks on the side. Be sure any spillway rocks are level. Photo by Eamonn Hughes

A stream can be constructed in fairly level ground. Simply have the bed lower one inch per ten linear feet from its head to its return point in the reservoir pond.

as the drop is higher than the water level in the channel below, you can use pieces of overlapping liner as in the waterfall construction. Stream sections are usually dug deepest at the entry point from the preceding section. Remember to consider the amount of water involved in your system and how it will impact the level of your reservoir pond. (Compute water volume in the system the same way you figure pond volume: length × width × depth for the cubic footage of water, then multiply that product by 7.5, the number of gallons of water in a cubic foot. To compute your stream system volume, use .25 for the depth

for 3 inches or one quarter of a foot of water.) Lowering the reservoir pond by one inch would be insignificant. A drop of several inches could jeopardize aquatic plants and would be unattractive.

Using preformed waterfall/stream units makes for some difficulty in concealing their prefabrication. Judicious use of rocks and plants can naturalize the construction.

General Pond Maintenance

Pond maintenance is based on both aesthetics and the creation

of a healthy environment for the goldfish you keep within it. Goldfish appreciate plants. Plants attract insects that supply welcome food to your fish as well as cover and protection from predators and harsh sunlight. The plants and fish in your pond coexist symbiotically.

All plants produce new foliage and blooms that die as fresh growth arrives. If you do not prune away the yellowing foliage and the spent blooms, they will fall to the pond bottom and gradually decompose, contributing to sedimentary buildup and the organic bio-load of the pond. This affects the water quality, impacting directly the life and health of your fish. (See Chapter 4.) Additionally, dying foliage attracts insects such as aphids that may further disfigure the plants. Keeping aged foliage pruned away keeps your pond looking beautiful.

While you perform certain maintenance regardless of the size or population of your pond, you can significantly lessen your workload by keeping your fish load low. The more fish loading, the more maintenance! As your fish load approaches the maximum stocking rate — one inch of goldfish per square foot of water surface — your maintenance routine significantly increases. Bio-filters become a necessity and they themselves require maintenance. By keeping your fish load low, you can rely on vegetable filtration and spend more

If your pond is not maximally stocked with fish, you can rely on plants (vegetable filtration) to remove excess nutrients from the water.

Maintenance of pond plants, such as this N. 'Mayla,' are part of goldfish pond care.

time enjoying rather than tending your pond.

Vegetable filtration involves floating aquatics such as water hyacinth, or submerged aquatics such as anacharis, or *Elodea canadensis*, that remove excess nutrients from the pond water. Other aquatic marginal plants, such as watercress, water celery, cattails, arrowhead, or pickerel weed, help with this task to a lesser degree. They can be grown in a stream bed or within a smaller pond, usually equal to ten percent of the main pond area, through which the pond water flows before returning to the main pond. (See Chapter 4.)

Seasonal Pond Maintenance

Spring

Because you cleaned your pond well in the autumn, you may not need to empty it now for a thorough cleaning. If, however, *any* amount of leaves and organic matter has accumulated on the bottom over the winter, treat the spring cleaning as you do your annual fall cleaning.

Your fish are emerging from hibernation over the cold winter months. In tropical zones, they are resuming a more active life than the slowed respite of winter. Before your fish begin active behavior, observe them closely for signs of parasites or disease that merit removing the afflicted ones to a hospital tank for treatment. This is the time of year when their immune systems are only beginning to awaken. Many pests and disease organisms awaken at lower temperatures and attack helpless and winter-weakened fish.

Once the water temperature has stabilized at 55°F or above, you can resume feeding. Be considerate of slowed digestive systems and feed easily digested food, such as wheat-germ–based food, Cheerios, or cooked spinach. You may wish to feed a medicated wheat-germ food for the first few weeks as disease prevention. After the water temperature has stabilized at 59°F, you can resume feeding the higher-protein foods of summer.

Even if you do not need to fully clean the pond, perform a partial water exchange of up to 40 percent of the pond volume. Remember to use dechlorinator if necessary. Monitor the water quality by testing weekly. Before the nitrogen cycle fully kicks in with warmer weather (it requires four to six weeks), you may see an ammonia spike and then a nitrite spike in the pond water. Both conditions

As your fish resume eating in the spring, be kind to their digestive systems and start them out with wheat-germ based foods until the water warms to 60°F.

should be monitored and treated as necessary. (See Chapter 4.)

Repot plants as needed. Wait until after bloom to repot spring-blooming plants such as water irises.

You may start up your bio-filter after the last ice has left the pond. Be sure it is cleaned and free of sediment from the previous season. Jump-start it with the inoculation you have kept going all winter (see Chapter 4) or with a commercial nitrifying bacteria product.

Your goldfish are likely to spawn as the water warms. Monitor your fish so none are beached by accident. Treat any abrasions or wounds that might occur in the activity. (See Chapter 5.)

Spring algae bloom may also occur as the water warms. Be patient. As your plants resume growth, they will begin removing more of the water's nutrients and will naturally starve the algae. As the algae die and collect on the pond bottom, remove the "dead bodies" with a skimmer net or a pond vac before they begin to decompose and negatively impact the water quality. If the algae bloom does not clear with the growth of your aquatic plants, check your fish load. You probably have too many fish for the pond.

Summer

Feed your goldfish high-protein food once or twice a day, always feeding only what they will consume in five to ten minutes. Net out any uneaten food to prevent the food from settling to the bottom and adding to the bio-load of the pond. Keep a submersible thermometer handy to monitor the water temperature approximately one-third of the way down into the water. If the water temperature hits 86°F, stop feeding your fish. Tropical ponds that normally attain such temperatures should be provided with shading or water exchanges to cool the water to below 86°F. Goldfish are a cool-water fish and will experience life-threatening stress in temperatures above 86°F sustained

over extended periods.

Either monitor the dissolved oxygen levels of the summer pond or carefully watch the behavior of your fish. Dissolved oxygen may be drastically lowered overnight, particularly in the presence of many plants or green-water algae. Warmer water holds less oxygen than cooler water. Occasional summer storms can cause the water to invert, the less-oxygenated waters coming to the top of your pond. Your fish will tell you if the oxygen is too low by congregating near oxygenated water sources, such as your waterfall entry. They might also gasp at the water's surface, especially early in the morning. Supply additional aeration by adding more moving water features to the pond or by using a long bar air stone sus-

Continue monitoring the water quality through the summer when heat and growing fish can affect it.

pended halfway down into the water.

As the spring babies grow, consider their impact on the fish loading of the pond. You may wish to net out many and find them new homes, either in a new pond of your own or a friend's or in a local pet store.

Each week, prune any yellowing foliage and spent blossoms from the pond.

Use a pond vac or swimming pool skimmer to control sedimentary buildup on the pond bottom. This can be performed with a weekly or biweekly five percent water exchange. Use a dechlorinator if you exchange more than five percent of the water volume.

Autumn

As temperatures begin to cool, switch to wheat-germ based foods and cut back on the amount of food offered. Often your fish will let you know how much they want. By the end of October in northern climates, you will be feeding only once or twice a week, completely stopping once the water temperature has stabilized below 55°F.

Perform a complete pond cleaning to prepare the pond for winter. Although netting the pond prevents leaves from accumulating on the pond bottom, ensure that a layer of sediment does not sit on the pond bottom through the winter. A layer of sediment would provide a winter home to both parasites and bacteria that can cause problems for your fish in very early spring. Prune off all foliage on plants that might decompose into the water. Water lilies are pruned and set in the deepest portion of the pond. Soft-stemmed plants with foliage that turns mushy, such as arrowhead and pickerel, should be fully cut back even though they can remain through the winter. Hard-stemmed plants, such as bulrushes and cattails, can wait for spring. Their stems protruding through the ice can assist with gas exchanges from the water during the winter. Tropical plants should be moved indoors before the first frost to prevent their dying. Tropical water lilies should experience at least one, if not two, hard frosts before being removed from the pond and their tubers stored.

Provide winter cover for your fish if predators might be a problem. Herons, for example, winter over in cold climates and will feed in your pond in the dead of winter. Set empty pots on their sides on the pond bottom to provide cover to the fish and to give them protection.

Clean and store pumps and filters if you will not run them

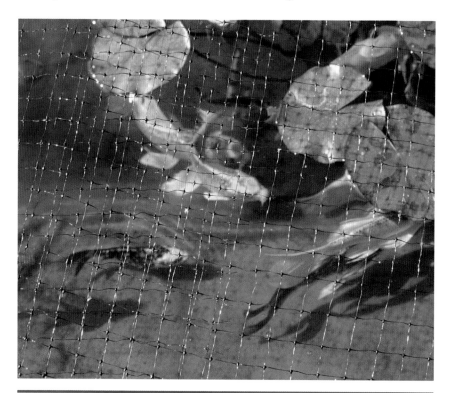

Erect bird netting over your autumn pond to prevent leaves from falling in and eventually fouling the water.

through the winter. Store oil-encapsulated pumps in a bucket of water to prevent their seals from drying out and possibly leaking the following year. Mag-drive pumps can be stored dry. If you have a bio-filter, clean its media before putting the filter in storage or use it to maintain the bacteria indoors over the winter. (See Chapter 4.)

Winter

In freezing zones, you'll want to keep a hole open in the ice to allow gas exchanges to occur. The biggest danger to fish in winter is that the pond will freeze over and hydrogen sulfide-producing organic debris will remain on the pond bottom. Without a hole to release this toxic chemical from the water, toxic gases in your pond may kill the fish. Even a hole left open may not be sufficient if the pond goes to bed for the winter in a filthy condition, especially if you are carrying a maximum fish load. Many

pondkeepers use floating pond de-icers or stocktank heaters to keep a small portion ice-free. You may also set your submersible pump at the water surface, where its bubbling will keep a hole open except in the coldest regions. Do not continue running a submersible pump in the lower third of the pond; doing so will cause the colder water at the surface to mix with the warmer water

If your winters are severe, you may wish to erect a greenhouse tent over your pond.

deeper in the pond, thereby cooling the water where your fish are "hibernating." The worst-case scenario is that the pond may freeze clear to the bottom. This same principle holds true for the use of air stones in the winter pond. Submerge air stones only within the upper third of the pond water. Better than nothing is to float rubber balls or sheets of Styrofoam on the pond.

In cold climates, do not feed your fish, even during the occasional warm spell. Their metabolisms are too slow to digest food properly. The food may sit too long in their intestines, and it will rot and invite bacteria to feast. Even if your fish are kept indoors in a greenhouse pond, test the water temperature to be sure it is over 55°F before feeding.

(For information on water chemistry, see Chapter 4. For information on fish health, see Chapter 5.)

CHAPTER THREE

The Koi Pond

The main attraction of a koi pond is the koi.

How often has the new pond owner trekked to the nearest pet shop to announce proudly, "I have a pond and I need some fish"? A smiling young salesclerk points the way: "Oh, you need some koi!" The new pondkeeper excitedly carts home three or four small koi of perhaps only three or four inches and places them within the new four- to six-foot-diameter pond. The fish grow…and grow…and grow. Within one season, they are 12 to 15 inches long! In the next seasons they may grow equally as much, to their mature length of 20 to 30 inches, or more. At this point, the realization hits: koi are not goldfish.

By this time, the new pond owner has also realized something else—those large fish are complicating what was supposed to be a quiet, tranquil gardening experience. They root around in plants, as all fish do, but these big babies end up tearing up the plants, eating the more tender ones, and uprooting any and all. With special care, koi can be kept in the typical two-foot-deep water garden. But is this the best way to keep koi?

Basic Components of Koi Ponds

Depth

A minimum depth of three feet is recommended for keeping koi. Four feet, or even up to six, is even better to accommodate the specific needs of your koi. koi are a cold-water fish. They do not like or survive healthily in water temperatures approaching 90°F. Such high temperatures are common to the two-foot-deep pond in the summer. Depths of three feet or more help buffer the water temperature and prevent life-threatening stress to the koi that comes with the plummeting oxygen-holding capacity of warmer water.

Space

Three or four times as large as mature goldfish, koi obviously need more space for proper swimming, exercise, and muscular development. While it may seem that fish spend their time cruising horizontally within the pond, they require vertical swimming as well for proper muscular development. The larger koi needs depth for this exercise.

Space involves not just habitation area; it also involves oxygen-holding capacity of the

Koi are not goldfish!

water. For that reason, the common stocking formula suggested for koi is one half inch of fish per square foot of water surface. In an 8' × 10' pond with 80 square feet of water surface, for example, you should stock only 40 inches of koi. This may mean only two koi! Once you approach that maximum stocking level, you must install a bio-filtration system that increases the stocking capacity for your pond. Likewise, you need also to install oxygen enhancements, such as venturi systems. Even with extra aeration, koi are simply not suitable in a small pond.

The larger size of koi mandates a larger pond for keeping them. Photo of the koi pond of the Weideners' of Louisville, Kentucky.

Koi enjoy basking beneath water-lily leaves, nibbling on tender submerged plants, and "rooting" in substrate for insect larvae. If your aquatic plants are solely for the benefit of your koi, you won't object to the uprooted or eaten plants. Many serious koi keepers do not keep their koi in planted ponds at all. A compromise is to install a dual-pond system with the aquatic plants kept in a separate but connected pond. Another alternative is to create planting pockets around the edge of the pond. These pockets are planted and filled to the water's surface with river rock or small cobbles that prevent the fish from getting into the plants. If very shallow water is allowed over the cobbles, fish fry may find safety, too.

While including plants in the koi pond provides cover for fish and fry, as well as a food source, the plants also use up nitrates that might otherwise foster algae blooms. However, during the day, plants use carbon dioxide to produce their food, giving off oxygen in the process of photosynthesis. At night, plants use oxygen and give off carbon dioxide during respiration. Carbon dioxide, in turn, becomes carbonic acid in the water, which can pull down the water's pH. A poorly buffered pond that includes plants can, therefore, experience great swings in pH.

(See Chapter 4.)

If you decide to keep plants in your koi pond, disinfect the new plants for parasites and diseases that might be transmitted to your pond fish. Use a 3 to 5 percent salt solution as a dip for several minutes, or dip the plants in a solution of one cup of vinegar mixed with a quart of water. Rinse the plants well before setting them within the pond.

Filtration

Overcrowding a pond accounts for perhaps 90 percent of all health problems with koi. Water quality declines rapidly when too many fish are crowded in too little water without enough surface area. Clear water, which is not necessarily indicative of good water quality, is desirable so fish can be observed and enjoyed. Water quality, however, includes invisible aspects of the water — the presence of ammonia, nitrite, and hydrogen sulfide, for example, or the lack of enough dissolved oxygen.

Like other fish, koi produce fecal waste and ammonia. If allowed to accumulate on the pond bottom, fecal waste fouls the water, as anaerobic bacteria reduce, rather than oxidize, the organic wastes. The by-product of this action is the deadly gas hydrogen sulfide. Ammonia,

Clear water can be deceptive. Unseen dangers to your fish are the presence of ammonia, nitrite, and hydrogen sulfide, or the lack of enough dissolved oxygen in the water. Photo of the koi pond of the Bushes, of Portland, Oregon.

entering the water from the gills and kidneys of the fish, can burn koi gills. Even more critical is nitrite. Nitrite occurs as bacteria oxidize the ammonia in the nitrogen cycle. Nitrite inhibits the blood from holding oxygen and results in the suffocation (death) of your fish.

A pond built specifically for koi, therefore, will have bottom drains to deal with the bottom wastes efficiently . The most efficient bottom-drain system covers perhaps ten square feet of the pond bottom. A 10' × 20' pond would have two bottom drains. Bottom drains are best installed with the initial pond installation, but the late Bob Spindola designed one for TetraPond that may be retrofitted after construction is com-

pleted. Bob Bon Giorno of Suburban Water Gardens has also designed a retrofitted bottom drain that is installed in the side wall of an existing pond. The use of bottom-drain circulation to continually pull organic settlement from the pond prevents conditions that produce hydrogen sulfide.

To protect fish from ammonia and nitrite, bio-filtration is used. Bio-filters provide a home for the beneficial, colonizing, nitrifying bacteria that work within the nitrogen cycle to convert ammonia into nitrite and then the nitrite into relatively harmless nitrate. Being aerobic bacteria, they require ample oxygen to perform their jobs. Traditional bio-filters for koi ponds were large,

usually one-third the size of the koi pond. In recent years, bio-filters have been developed that offer more living space for the bacteria in far less space. The vortex system uses the chamber design to provide particulate settlement and bio-filtration in sequence. Bubble-bead and fluid-bed filters suspend the bio-media in constantly moving water to promote a high degree of conversion of ammonia and nitrite. These filters require backwashing to rid them of particulate matter. (See Chapter 4.) Either of these systems requires that the pond water be pumped through the bio-filter.

Because bio-filtration allows a significant increase in the fish load of the pond, the system is run 24 hours a day. Shutting down the system even for brief periods can be disastrous in a maxed-out pond. Keeping a generator on hand for emergencies may save your fish. Likewise, many pondkeepers keep a back-up pump on hand. Always use a swing check valve between the intake opening of the pump and the pump in case the power shuts off. This will stop the backward flow of water that can drain the system. Avoid using in-line spring check valves, as they clog and are difficult to clean.

Whatever the style of filter system you use, it will require some space. If you are fortunate to have a garage nearby, a des-

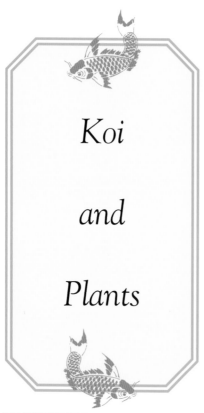

Koi

and

Plants

Enclosing your plant pots within netting keeps koi from rooting around in the gravel topping and uprooting plants.

The roots of floating aquatics are delicious fodder for your koi. Protect the plants with floating net enclosures.

Creating shallow cobble-filled planting pockets at the edge of the pond edge allows koi and plants to be kept safely in the same pond.

Special side hangers avoid the shallow planting shelves that invite predators to feast in your pond.

Steve Childers, president of the Oklahoma Koi Society, sets an emergent lotus plant in the corner of his koi pond for safekeeping.

ignated corner may house the system. An attractive housing, such as a replica of a grist mill, might be another option. Most koi pondkeepers simply hide the system behind an attractive fence, around the corner of the house, or behind landscaping. Fortunately, the system need not be immediately adjacent to the pond.

A fluid-bed bio-filter provides a chamber in which very small media are kept in suspension. It is backwashed to clean it of particulate matter.

A vortex-chamber filtration system involves the use of separate vats for particulate settlement and bio-filtration.

Beneficial Bacteria for Your Koi Pond

Starting up a bio-filter takes time. It may take several weeks for the beneficial aerobic bacteria to establish. These bacteria are primarily *Nitrosomonas* and *Nitrobacter* that work within the naturally occurring nitrogen cycle in the water. Ammonia that can burn fish gills is produced as waste by both fish and plant decomposition; it is oxidized by *Nitrosomonas* bacteria. The by-product of this action is nitrite, which can harm your fish even in a small quantity by preventing blood from carrying oxygen. *Nitrobacter* bacteria oxidize the deadly nitrite. The by-product of that action is relatively harmless nitrate. You can monitor this invisible process by testing your water once you have started up your bio-filter. Initially, you will note a spike in ammonia. Monitor this and take appropriate measures if the spike is high enough to jeopardize your fish. A few weeks later, you will note a spike in nitrite. Again, take appropriate steps if necessary.

(See Chapter 4.) Finally, a few more weeks later, you will note no ammonia or nitrite presence in the water. Instead, you may register the presence of nitrate. Providing a few water hyacinths in the top of your bio-filter minimizes the nitrate.

By "seeding" the bio-filter, the process may be quickened to two or three weeks before the filter may be considered established. Many products are available to do this, some in freeze-dried form and some in liquid suspension. Controversy still exists on the use and methodology of these products. Some experts suggest that aerobic bacteria can live within an enclosed bottle for only two weeks. Others swear that freeze-dried bacteria are not as viable. Worse yet, some experts suggest that the bacteria do not work at all! The consensus of opinion is, however, that the bacteria do enhance the nitrogen cycle. Whatever form you use, monitor your pond water with daily testing to assure yourself that the cycle is being implemented.

Recently, a sludge-eating bacteria product has hit the marketplace. This product consists of *Bacillus subtilis*, which is actually an aerobic bacteria. Because these bacteria are added to the new nitrifying bacteria products, they are ensured of the necessary oxygen for their work. Dr. Erik L.

A bio-filter system properly sized to your pond provides your fish with clean safe water.

Johnson, known as "koivet" at his Internet site, reports a controlled study he performed using the sludge-digesting bacteria. Over a period of several weeks, the solid waste was reduced by 700 percent. If you have an effective bottom drain and do not allow solid wastes to collect within your pond's water system, your pond is not likely to need the services of *Bacillus subtilis*. However, if your pond is collecting a thin layer of organic sediment on the bottom or within the stream or filtration system, *Bacillus subtilis* could be most beneficial. Remember that aerobic bacteria work only on the surface layer of submersed sediment exposed to oxygenated water. Down in the depths, bacteria are anaero-

bically reducing matter and producing hydrogen sulfide.

Other Water Quality Concerns

Koi are a cool-water fish that enjoy their best health in temperatures ranging from 50° to 78°F. Higher temperatures produce stress, and lower temperatures send a koi into a hibernation state in which its immune system shuts down, leaving the fish vulnerable to attack by disease and parasites. The stress of higher temperatures also affects the immune system of the koi , causing the fish to slough off the protective slime coating. koi are not fed in

either extreme of their optimum temperature range. Water temperatures in excess of 90°F warrant an immediate water exchange of 25 to 30 percent. While water depth provides a buffer to temperature extremes, a lattice pergola or shade cloth over the pond protects the pond from intense sunlight and heat.

Water pH should be in the range of 6.8 to 7.8. koi survive quite healthily in water stabilized at pH readings in the low-eight range, too. Likewise, moderately hard water of 200 milligrams per liter of calcium carbonate is healthy for koi. Acidic water presents major problems, as naturally ensuing pH swings are very stressful. Keep the pH and hardness of

A shade cloth cover over the koi pond protects it from high temperatures and intense sunlight.

your water consistent. That's more important than constantly changing the water chemistry to achieve a particular goal. (See Chapter 4.)

The Pump

In selecting the pump that runs your filtration system, look for an energy-efficient pump since you will run the system around the clock. Remember that during the nighttime hours oxygen levels tend to drop,

Koi pond filtration systems require high-capacity pumps. These are usually cost-efficient out-of-pond pumps.

especially if plants are present in the pond, making the oxygenation supplied by a return waterfall or venturi system critical to the health of your fish. Out-of-pond pumps tend to be less expensive to operate, especially in the sizes needed for the volume of water usually involved in a koi pond. Your

pump should be able to pump your pond's volume at least once every three hours. A 10' × 20' pond with four feet of depth contains 6,000 gallons, for example. (Length × width × depth × 7.5 gallons in a cubic foot = pond volume.) To turn over 6,000 gallons once every three hours, you would need a pump capable of pumping 2,000 gallons per hour. Submersible water-garden pumps are cost-effective only to the 1,200-gallons-per-hour size.

UV Lights

A by-product of the newer, high-efficiency bio-filtration systems is the proliferation of green-water algae. Since ultraviolet light kills this single-celled plant, along with unwanted bacteria and microscopic organisms that might prove harmful to the fish, UV attachments are commonly used with koi ponds. UV units contain a special lightbulb that is located inside a long, thin glass tube known as a quartz sleeve. This allows the UV bulb to operate both dry and hot. The bulb should not come into contact with the much cooler pond water. Many koi keepers have found that halving the manufacturer's recommended flow rate of water past the UV bulb is most effective.

Ultraviolet light is radiated

Ultraviolet attachments to the filtration system keep the water free of single-celled, green-water algae and microscopic organisms.

at energy levels rated in microwatts per second. The two factors that influence the effectiveness of ultraviolet light in disinfecting are water flow (exposure time) and water clarity. The amount of time needed for destruction of the microorganism is based on microwatts per second of exposure. It's important to know the total amount of microwatts produced by the lamp. Select a UV unit with a germicidal level of effectiveness of 253.7 nanometers.

Water clarity is very important to attain the necessary exposure time since the light must penetrate the water flowing past it. The recommended turnover rate of the pond volume is a maximum of once per hour and a minimum of once every three hours. A 6,000-gallon koi pond with a turnover rate of once every two hours would require a pump capable of pumping 3,000 gallons per hour, or 50 gallons per minute. You would then select and fit your UV to attain a one-second exposure to the water flow.

In setting up a UV light, install it in-line after the bio-filter, so the water is cleanest. Likewise, keep the lightbulb clean because dirt obviously reduces efficiency. Change the bulb every spring since its efficiency is reduced before it burns out. Don't run the UV until the bio-filter is up and running so you do not kill good bacteria. Attach all electrical wiring to a ground-fault interrupter circuit.

Skimmer System

Yet another part of the filtration system commonly supplied to dedicated koi ponds is a skimmer system. The skimmer system of a koi pond is set up at the surface of the water to capture any floating debris that might fall into the pond. It is set up near the edge of the pond so it can be easily cleaned from the side of the pond. A small

Dedicated koi ponds often use a skimmer system to remove pollen and other debris that might fall on the pond's surface.

The skimmer system includes an easily removed basket that traps surface debris.

skimmer basket, much like a swimming pool skimmer unit, is contained within the unit. Pollen, leaves, and other particulate debris move into the basket before they can submerge and drift to the pond bottom, where they would add to the bio-load. These skimmer systems are much safer for your koi than the common skimmer system sometimes constructed outside and adjacent to the water garden. The water-garden skimmer system includes a submersible pump within the unit that can injure or kill very small fish.

Venturi System

A venturi system is simply a means of adding additional oxygen to the water. It forces air into the koi pond below the water level so that an effervescent flow of air bubbles travels up through the pond water. Large koi ponds may have several venturis in operation. Especially if the fish load in your koi pond is near the maximum loading level, monitor the dissolved oxygen level available for your koi. koi should have over 7 ppm of dissolved oxygen—the more, the better. At even 5 ppm, they may experience stress as well a loss of color intensity. At 3 ppm, they won't live long.

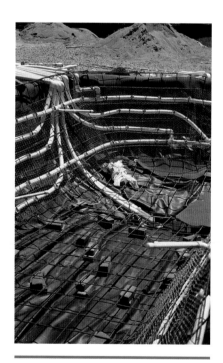

Koi pond venturi systems are a much larger version of the popular aquarium aeration device.

Koi ponds of cement or fiberglass involve highly complicated construction that requires considerable expertise. Information on such construction is available from the Associated Koi Clubs of America.

Building the Koi Pond

Siting

Koi are often called "living jewels." With myriad colors and patterns, magnificent size, and distinctive personalities, these special fish deserve a pond near the house, where they can be most fully enjoyed. Make the pond readily accessible, too, so that tending the fish is easy. An ideal location for the koi pond is near your home but underneath an outdoor roof. This will allow you to enjoy them even on rainy days. Outdoor furnishings are an important addition to your koi pond because you will spend many hours there. A solid or lattice roof over the pond serves other important functions, too. Herons flying overhead are not likely to spot your colorful fish. The shelter also protects the pond from bright sunlight, which fades the fish's color, overheats the water, and fosters algae blooms that cloud and obscure the water. A dedicated koi pond becomes the focal point of a lanai or pergola. koi ponds that will include plants should be sited where they can receive at least three hours of direct sunlight each day, for the sake of the plants.

The Liner

As with the goldfish/water garden pond, select a liner membrane that will last for years. Roofing rubber may be cured with toxic chemicals or dusted with toxic talc. A 45-mil EPDM liner should last many years in your pond, although you may wish to indulge in the thicker 60-mil as extra assurance. Even the koi pond made of concrete may use the EPDM underneath the cement as a precaution against cracks and leaks. Commercial bottom-drain kits are available that make installation through flexible membranes a simple and safe process.

The Plumbing

Remember that rigid white PVC is potable and black is not. Potable simply means that the water is safe for human consumption. This makes it desirable also for finned pets. Flexible black piping is also potable. If you wish to camouflage white piping, paint or wrap it.

Before installing your koi pond, you need to have your plumbing firmly in mind. While you can design a koi pond that uses a submersible pump, it is more likely that you will want a pond large enough to keep several koi. This is likely to hold several thousand gallons. Turning such a volume over once every two or three hours usually involves an out-of-pond external pump. You will need piping to go from the pond to the pump and filter system. You may have a line feeding from the bottom drain to the pump and a return feed line. Depending on the size of the pond, there may be several such lines. You will also have several lines at the pump and filter system directing water to the filter, through the UV attachment and returns. Each line should have valves affixed in-line both to control the flow as well as to shut down and by-pass any of its operations. Medicating the pond, for example, usually involves bypassing the bio-filter to avoid killing off the nitrifying bacteria. Looking at such setups can be dauntingly confusing! But consider it practically: Carry water from the pond to the pump, shunt it to the filter system and through the UV attachment, and return it cleansed to the pond. Avoid elbows whenever possible, as they will slow the flow of water and can collect air bubbles at their peaks, inhibiting filter function. Elbows from the bottom drain can become clogged.

Unless you are a would-be engineer, consult an experienced person to design and install your plumbing system. Contacting a koi club can help. Manufacturers and retailers of full systems can also guide you.

Chances are that you will use more than one pump within your total system: a pump dedicated to your filtration system and another dedicated to extra water features, all of which require plumbing.

Siting your koi pond near your house allows you to readily enjoy your water pets and tend to them.

Construction

The lined koi pond is constructed much the same as the goldfish/water garden described in Chapter 2, but deeper. A koi pond must be at least or three feet deep. Many lined koi ponds offer two depths, one at the three-foot level and a deeper portion at five or six feet; some are even eight feet deep. The bottom of your excavation should slope toward the sump area where you will install the bottom drains; one drain should service every 10 to 15 square feet.

Before setting in the liner, install the plumbing lines. Be absolutely certain that your liner accurately fits the excavation, as your bottom drain will protrude through the liner. Once you have cut through the liner, the placement is permanent! Patching and sealing pieces of rubber liner may not be effective over a period of years, especially if you do the patching yourself. As a precaution, you may wish to compute the size of liner and add an extra foot all the way around, rather than the extra six inches around that is normally computed for the goldfish/water garden.

If you intend to include plants in your koi pond, consider using plant pedestals or side-hooking hangers for the plant pots. This allows you to

Shallow, rock-lined ponds are not the best environment for your koi.

avoid shallow planting shelves, which offer predators easy access to your koi.

For the safety of your koi, do not use rocks on the liner inside the pond. Particularly during the rigors of spawning, your fish may injure themselves on rocks. Using rocks within

the pond also complicates maintenance as they impede the flow of sedimentary wastes into the bottom drain and allow sedimentary buildup that results in production of toxic hydrogen sulfide.

Keep your pond design simple. Avoid coves and dead-

A dual-pond construction allows you to keep plants in one pond and koi in the connecting pond.

Dual-Pond Koi Pond Construction

Constructing a dual pond allows you to enjoy the best of both worlds: an upper pond for aquatic plants and a lower pond dedicated to your koi. The drop between the two pond excavations may be only several inches, with a small spillway connecting the two. Water returns from your filtration system to the top of the upper plant pond. On a fairly level site, concrete building blocks can define your excavated form and establish the needed elevation change.

Charles Phelps, a prominent koi hobbyist in Louisville, Kentucky, is understandably proud of his koi selections.

water areas. Curved perimeters allow better water flow. Even if the upper edge has corners, consider curving them within the pond.

Depending on the soil type in your area, you may need to supply a wooden form or concrete blocks inside the excavation to protect the integrity of the pond over time.

Be sure the upper edge of the pond is stabilized so the heavy rocks that form the edge will not settle. Over the course of time, many people will visit your pond, so make sure all edging is secure and not at risk of falling into the pond. Retrieving edging is a chore, and falling rocks are a hazard to your koi.

Selecting Your Koi

Should you find yourself with many koi for your selection, you may find yourself wanting one of each! koi are available in innumerable color patterns, with scales or without (*doitsu*), with plain colors or with metallic sheens to their scales. There is even a whole Japanese vocabulary to describe all their color variations. However, unless you intend to become a serious hobbyist who shows your pets, you should select koi that please you. A freckle-faced koi, for example, won't win show awards or even be acknowledged as a koi by the elitist, but it may present so

much personality that you love it. If you like it, buy it....and name it, and love it.

You will probably start out with relatively small koi. Even good-quality koi are relatively inexpensive at small sizes because their color and pattern development are unpredictable. While you can focus on the more defined patterns and more vibrant colors, you cannot be sure they will remain so. The late Bob Spindola counseled, "Buy for the black and bet on the red." Black patterns are evidenced in young fish. The black often appears grayish just below the skin surface. It will rise up with vibrancy as the fish ages. Red coloration is more unpredictable; the color fades and the pattern blurs out. This is part of the enjoyment of koi. They change from year to year, only stabilizing somewhat in maturity when size alone decrees a much higher price tag.

To begin your koi adventure, select healthy fish. Your selection should have both eyes and all of its fins. The eyes should be clear and not cloudy, popped out, or recessed into the head. The fins should not be frayed or blushed pink. Both sets of barbels should be present around the koi's mouth. The gills should be pink, not red or white, and the gill plates should cover the gills completely. The fish should have no wounds or blood spots on its body. Likewise, there should be no raised scales or strange bumps or bulges on its body. Its back should be straight, not kinked or indented. The body should bear a slight bulge outward with the sides, top, and bottom slightly concave. It should swim easily in a straight line.

If you envision yourself becoming very serious about koi keeping, contact the Associated Koi Clubs of America, or a similar organization, to acquire detailed and specific information on koi health, nutrition, pond construction, and filters. Often, dedicated koi ponds are of cement or fiberglass with quite elaborate plumbing. While you can build such ponds yourself, expert help is required! Being knowledgeable of such methods enables you, too, to hire the best builder. For the rest of us enthusiastic hobbyists who want only to provide a proper home to special koi pets, look at koi pond construction with rubber liners.

Spawning

Even if you decide not to breed your koi, they will still spawn. Spawning is a vigorous activity in the pond. For that reason, no sharp edges or rocks are allowed in the koi pond. Even edging rocks are placed a few inches above the water level to ensure that the koi do not injure themselves. A simple scrape or cut incurred during spawning invites fungus and bacterial infections that can kill your fish.

Likewise, the spawning activity results in a protein overload in the pond. This is evidenced by a foamy or sudsy appearance on the water. The protein joins the nitrogen cycle of the pond and ammonia spikes occur. Even as the ammonia spikes jeopardize the koi's health, the ensuing nitrite spike can kill them. Water exchanges, up to 40 percent, can be critical at these times.

Koi mating begins in spring as days lengthen and tempera-

Sticky eggs cling to nylon spawning fibers set within the koi pond.

tures rise. The change in water temperature seems to be the trigger. Many people note that water changes or moving koi into new quarters triggers spawning.

The breeding usually begins in early morning, although you may not notice the behavior until later in the day. The female fish bears a noticeably swollen belly. One or more male koi begin following her, nudging her body with their noses. What appears to be mere bumping in spawning goldfish becomes a world wrestling event among the koi within your pond. The strong nudges by the males force the eggs from the female's anal opening. The males then simultaneously release their milt to fertilize the eggs. Very sticky, the eggs adhere to pond walls or to whatever they touch. They will hatch in four to seven days when the water temperature ranges between 65 and 72. Many koi keepers use spawning mats, ropes of frayed material, or even floating water hyacinths for the koi to deposit the eggs upon. The eggs can then be removed from the pond before the adults eat them. (Don't be surprised, however, if several weeks later you notice a few tiny fry swimming about in your pond!) If the eggs will be preserved for hatching elsewhere, be sure the hatchery water is well oxygenated and clean.

Because hundreds and hundreds of eggs are produced, the vast majority of which turn out to be "pet-quality" fish, breeders go through a series of cullings to discard the fry deemed to offer the least possibility of prime development. As a pet-owner with a spawning of hundreds of baby fish, you may find you have nowhere to put all those babies. Many hobbyist koi keepers go through only one hatching before deciding to simply discard the eggs before they can hatch. Chuck Mulford, a koi hobbyist in Atlanta, actually lowers the water in his koi pond after spawning to dry up the eggs deposited on the pond walls.

Feeding Your Koi

Because koi, like other fish, function with a metabolism based on the surrounding water, your feeding is dependent on water temperature. This governs not only how much you feed; it also dictates what you feed. koi, after all, have no true stomach. Instead, much like a cow, they possess a very long intestinal tract that digests their food, which makes them "grazers." You will notice koi constantly nuzzling among plants or around the bottom of the pond, a natural behavior in quest for food. Particularly in the dedicated koi pond in which

Wally and Nancy Oyler join Rachel Hunter in Louisville, Kentucky, to share feeding time with the Hunters' award-winning koi.

Training your koi to eat from a floating ring makes it easier to net out uneaten food and prevents the floating food from being sucked into the skimmer basket.

It's a fact: koi love watermelon. String slices together to more easily remove the rinds when the koi have finished eating. Photo of indoor koi pond at Gotcha Koi in Ranier, Oregon.

other food sources such as insect larvae and tender plant growth are not available, it is important to feed your koi in several small feedings throughout the day. In the summer, as long as the water temperature is not above 85°F, feed your koi at least twice a day. Feed them what they will eat in only five minutes and then net out any remaining food to prevent it from eventually sinking to the bottom of the pond and adding to the pond's bio-load.

The lack of a true stomach in fish indicates that their foods are naturally digested in a waterlogged state. Dry foods can actually absorb moisture from the fish itself and cause intestinal blockages or constipation. Especially during low-temperature feedings in spring and autumn, soak all dry foods for 10 minutes before feeding them to your fish.

During cold-water periods when the water temperature is stabilized below 55°F, do not feed your koi at all. With their metabolisms so slowed, they cannot digest it properly. Food cannot pass through the intestines quickly enough, and it will begin to rot. This can produce blockages that threaten the health of your koi. Rotting food is also a beacon for bacteria. Bacteria attacking food within the fish's intestines can cause serious disease. Also keep in mind that unrefrigerated fish food has a shelf life of only six months; store leftovers in the freezer.

Similarly, when the water temperature ranges between 50° to 59°F, the intestinal tract of a koi is sluggish. During those early autumn and spring periods, feed easily digestible foods, such as waterlogged wheat-germ–based pellets, Cheerios, or vitamin-rich leafy-green vegetables, such as cooked spinach, or peas. (Lettuce is notoriously deficient in nutrition.) Chopped earthworms are a good source of protein for koi during these slow times, too. In the spring, feed sparingly until the bio-filter is functioning, since eating causes more ammonia and solid waste production by the fish. Dr. Erik Johnson, the Internet "koivet," recommends closing and opening koi feeding seasons with medicated food that helps prevent bacterial infections. Oxolinic acid is the proprietary ingredient in many of these foods.

During the autumn feeding, your koi may increase their weight by 20 percent. This stored fat is used throughout the winter hibernation when the water temperature is below 50°F. By spring, this fat reserve has been depleted and the koi appear noticeably thinner. If you feel compelled to feed them as the temperatures start to warm, start with leafy vegetables. Do not feed until the water has warmed to the 50°- to 55°F range.

Water temperatures in the 60°- to 85°F range encourage activity in your koi and the need for foods higher in proteins. Some of these foods contain color enhancers or spirulina algae products. While they can benefit the koi's color, too much can cause white colors to turn yellowish. Soak dry pellets, keeping in mind that smaller pellets cause fewer digestive problems than larger ones. If you must feed koi an inexpensive chow, go for catfish chow rather than trout chow, which is too fatty and oily. Prolonged feeding of trout chow can lead to fatty liver disease. The oiliness of trout chow also leaves a film on your pond's surface, adding to the bio-load and disrupting the critical oxygen exchange at the pond's surface.

Koi appreciate variety in their diets just as we do. Fresh fruit and vegetables are welcome summer treats. When you gather in the backyard to celebrate the Fourth of July, don't forget to cut a few extra slices of watermelon to toss in the koi pond. Your pets will enjoy the treat, but you'll have to net out the seeds they spit out.

Feeding Rates and Water Temperatures

Consider a feeding ration to be the amount the koi eat within five minutes. A half-rate ration would be what they eat in two and a half minutes.

The water temperature is determined by submerging a thermometer to a one-third depth within the pond water.

Below 50°F: Don't feed, no matter how coyly they ask.

50°–55°F: Half ration every other day of wheat-germ–based foods and cooked leafy vegetables.

55°–60°F: Half ration every day; begin adding protein-based food.

60°–65°F: Feed a full ration of protein-based food once per day.

65°–84°F: Feed full rations of protein-based foods 2 or 3 times per day.

Supplement feedings with fresh fruit and vegetables.

85°F and above: Stop feeding until temperature stabilizes below 85°F.

Koi Pond Maintenance

Water Exchanges

Weekly water exchanges are important for the koi pond. These may be performed as part of your regular maintenance of the filtration system in which backwashing removes particulate matter along with water from the system. Remove and replace 5 to 25 percent of the pond's volume. If your water is treated with chlorine, be sure to treat exchanges greater than five percent with dechlor.

Many koi keepers who use large quantities of dechlor keep a supply of sodium thiosulfate on hand to mix their own dechlor. Sodium thiosulfate is available in quartzlike crystals. You need a scale to weigh them for a proper 130 grams per liter of water or 500 grams per gallon of water for a 13 percent solution. Add two drops of solution per gallon of pond volume. After figuring the dosage required for your pond, measure the drops in a clear measuring cup and record the figure where it can be easily referenced.

You will also perform a water exchange if the water

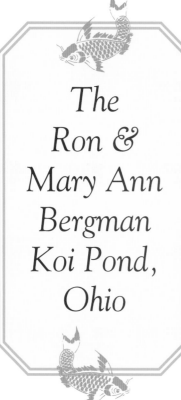

The Ron & Mary Ann Bergman Koi Pond, Ohio

The Bergmans' elaborate koi pond includes an entertainment gazebo and two koi ponds connected by a stream.

A unique waterfall flows into the upper pond from the base of the gazebo.

The shallow exit from the upper pond into the stream prevents the koi from swimming downstream.

temperature rises to 85°F. A 25 percent exchange of the total pond volume brings the temperature back into a safe range for your fish. If you live in a region with very hot summers and the water temperature frequently attains such high temperatures, consider adding shade protection to the pond.

Water exchanges of up to 40 percent are also used following spawning and when water testing denotes the presence of ammonia or nitrite.

Water Testing

Test your pond water every week! Monitor the pH of the water and check for the presence of ammonia and nitrite. Nitrate should also be checked, particularly if the pond has no plants to help with its removal. (See Chapter 4.)

Using Salt in the Koi Pond

The use of salt in the dedicated koi pond is the one defining criteria differentiating it from a water garden with plants. Most plants object to the presence of salt. Some plants such as cattails and water hyacinths will tolerate some brackishness, but submerged grasses and many water lilies will yellow and die. By the same token, koi are not salt-water fish, and you will not keep a constant salt dosage in the koi pond year-round.

Salt serves specific purposes within the koi pond. It does not evaporate, so over time your pond may become brackish. You must dilute and remove salt through water exchanges.

Gary Cryer and Bill Hawk of Koi of Oklahoma maintain an indoor koi pond for their special, imported koi.

If you use salt in your koi pond, have a salt tester to verify the percentage present at any time. Too much is not good at all. A three percent salt solution accomplishes the following:

1. Salt kills all parasites except encysted forms of ich. It is particularly useful in the low-temperature waters of autumn through spring when the immune systems of fish are either low or not functioning.

2. Salt stimulates production of the slime coat of the fish, the site of the immune system of enzymes that fight bacteria and parasites. Under stress, fish slough off their protective slime coating. This is sometimes detectable by the presence of a slippery white film on the water surface. Salt, therefore, is known as a tonic for stress.

3. Salt reduces water influx into the stressed fish by equalizing the osmolality of the fish and its surrounding water. This osmoregulatory capacity of salt is yet another reason why it is known as a tonic for stress.

4. Salt inhibits the uptake of nitrites by fish and in conjunction with water exchanges is the remedy for nitrite presence in water. Since nitrite also stresses the fish, the salt is doubly helpful.

5. Salt is beneficial for short-term applications, for example during transit. Salt inhibits the effects of ammonia in the water that might burn the fish's gills. Transport is stressful to fish, and the salt is a tonic.

Pond Closing

Autumn pond cleaning is the most critical maintenance job of koi keeping. Any time after the beginning of November, remove the pond cover netting that has been preventing leaves from blowing into the pond. Pump and empty your pond so only enough water is left to cover the fish. Remove any aquatic plants and store them for the winter. Clean away any leaves or sedimentary debris

Joe Zuritsky, owner of Quality Koi Company in Philadelphia, Pennsylvania, keeps special koi pets in a pond just outside his office.

The Koi Pond

A sheltered seating area next to the koi pond invites relaxing time with your pets.

A zigzag wooden bridge and stepping stones lend an Asian design to this New York Koi pond.

A small Texas backyard uses its entire area for a koi pond. The pond is accessed by low-maintenance deck surrounds.

from the pond bottom and sides. Allowing this to remain on the pond bottom through the winter provides a home for parasites and bacteria that will attack your weakened fish in the early spring before their immune systems have resumed. This debris also continues being reduced by anaerobic bacteria at low temperatures; the byproduct is toxic hydrogen sulfide. If the pond bottom is particularly dirty, remove your fish to temporary quarters as you clean, and avoid stirring up the deadly gas. Move them into covered quarters with dechlorinated water, preferably their own pond water, of the same temperature. The portable koi tanks used at koi shows are especially useful for this.

As you resume pumping out the remaining water, begin adding new water at the same time so the water level never drops below what is needed to fully cover the fish. Add dechlor as necessary to avoid stressing and harming the fish. If any sediment remains in the water, agitate it. Maintain the water level at this low point, pumping out and adding in at the same rate, until the water is cleared of all particulate matter that would eventually settle on the pond bottom.

You can then refill the pond to its normal level, adding dechlor as you go. Once the pond is refilled, add one pound of non-iodized salt for each 100 gallons of pond volume. Over the next two days, repeat the one percent addition of dissolved salt to the pond so that you have a three percent salt level in the pond to face the lowering temperatures. Place a floating de-icer in the pond and replace the pond cover net to prevent additional leaves from blowing in. Stop feeding your fish once the water temperature is consistently below 55°F.

Remove any bio-media, clean, and store, or use it to keep an inoculation alive for the spring pond. Continue operating your filtration system through the winter without its bio-media.

Heating the Winter Koi Pond

If your pond is at least 3 to 4 feet deep, you do not need to supply a heater to the koi pond. Your koi will simply hibernate or rest in the clean pond you have provided for their winter rest. If you do provide heat to the winter pond, however, avoid placing heaters in the bottom of the pond; doing so can set up convectional currents that lift the warmer water. It will chill as it rises toward the surface, returning colder water to the bottom and the koi. For the same reason, do not maintain any aeration device or submersible pump near the bottom. Place the heater within the filter system, preferably in the settling chamber, that you will keep running without filter media throughout the winter. Any heating unit should be thermostatically controlled and capable of maintaining the water temperature at a minimum of 60°F, even through the severest of winters. Rapidly fluctuating temperatures or

temperatures too high for proper hibernation but too low for safe feeding can be injurious to the health of koi. Furthermore, at temperatures below 50°F, the koi immune system does not function, but bacteria in the water are still active. If your heater cannot do a proper job through the winter, use it only to stabilize fluctuating spring and autumn temperatures.

The Koi Pond in Winter

In tropical and warm-weather climates, you can maintain your koi pond as per the dictates of the water temperature. You may select autumn, winter, or spring as your annual pond-cleaning time.

For cold-climate ponds, winter offers a season of all but benign neglect. You won't feed your fish. You won't disturb them at all, to avoid stressing them during this period of inactive immune systems. Since cooler water holds more oxygen than warmer water, the oxygen levels of the winter pond are likely to be fine for the pond not overly stocked with fish. If your fish load is beyond the maximum for your pond, you may wish to supply additional aeration through the winter. Supply aeration, however, in the upper third of the pond only, to avoid lowering the temperature of the deeper water where your koi take their quiet nap.

Disconnect the bottom drain to prevent returning chilled water in the waterfall from affecting the temperature of the pond. Failure to do so will lower the pond temperatures and risk the health of your fish. If you have a second pump that runs your waterfall, turn off the waterfall and bypass the water directly to the pond to avoid chilling it. Waterfalls that continue to run throughout the winter in freezing climates acquire significant ice sculptures, beautiful to look at but deceptive in their ability to siphon off water without your knowledge. If your bio-filter is not in line with the bottom drain or if it can be run from another water source in the upper half of your pond, you can continue running it through the winter, although without its bio-media. Insulate such systems with straw to prevent their freezing. (Note that straw will probably attract mice!) Clean and store any unused pumps or water features. Submersible, oil-encapsulated pumps should be stored in a bucket of water to prevent their seals from drying and leaking oil in your pond in the next season. Mag-drive pumps can be stored dry.

If your region experiences rains or snows during the winter, lower the pond level by two or three inches to allow for their accumulations. Use a floating livestock heater or a floating pond heater to keep a hole open in the ice. The primary reason for this is to allow a point of exchange for toxic hydrogen sulfide that might be produced from any decom-

Using brick terraces and wooden decks, all maintenance in this backyard is devoted to the koi pond.

A garden designed for wheelchair accessibility includes a koi pond.

posing matter remaining on the pond bottom. Keep a protective netting over the pond to prevent leaves and debris from entering the pond. The netting should be suspended above the pond so it doesn't touch the water. If it did, it might permit leaves to decompose and foul the water, and your fish could become entangled in it and tear their scales.

Use your water test kit occasionally during the winter to be sure ammonia is not accumulating in the water. Allow the sample to warm to room temperature to ensure an accurate test reading. You will not notice any nitrite presence since the bacteria that convert ammonia into nitrite are not active below 50°F. The primary source of ammonia in the winter pond is occasional feeding on warm days. (Another reason not to feed your koi during their winter hibernation!)

Koi Pond Seasonal Checklist

Spring

POND MAINTENANCE
*Follow the thorough pond-cleaning guidelines of autumn if

necessary. Be sure that no sediment accumulates on the pond bottom.
*Execute a 25 to 40 percent water change, using dechlor as necessary.
*Treat freshened water with a one percent salt dosage. (One pound of non-iodized salt per 100 gallons.) Test the salt level to determine how much more salt you need to add to bring the water to a three percent treatment. Apply salt dosages in

Plant filtration is supplied in a separate portion of this koi pond design.

one percent increments every 12 to 24 hours until a three percent level is achieved.

WATER QUALITY
*Restore biological filters to full activity and add commercial nitrifying bacteria or your own jump-start bacterial soup. (See Chapter 4.)
*Monitor ammonia and nitrite levels with a water test kit. Daily water changes up to 40% may be necessary if tests so indicate.

FEEDING
*Feed wheat-germ–based foods in water temperatures of 55° to 59°F.
*Feed medicated food for the first two or three weeks.
*Do not feed food leftover from the previous year unless it has been frozen or is less than six months old.

HEALTH
*While your fish are still sluggish, check them carefully for signs of parasites or disease. Remove affected fish to a quarantine tank for treatment.
*The salt treatment of the pond will be effective for most health problems. You can use a commercial product, following manufacturers' instructions, if desired.

Summer

POND MAINTENANCE
*Continue weekly water exchanges of 5 to 20 percent,

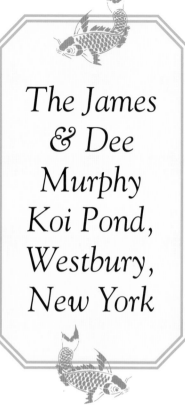

The James & Dee Murphy Koi Pond, Westbury, New York

A shallow planting pocket on the pond's edge is home to lovely lotus.

Built adjacent to a wooden, ground-level decking, this deep koi pond has clear and clean water.

Pennywort and parrot's feather provide nutrient removal in the waterfall return area as landscape color frames the pond.

The Koi Pond

CHAPTER FOUR

Water Quality and Pond Filtration

The pond you create in your backyard is not like the "open systems" found in nature.

As soon as you include living creatures within your pond, water quality becomes critically important. This involves far more than maintaining clear water in which to see and enjoy your aquatic pets. Suddenly, you need to know about water chemistry—the unseen world of your pets' watery habitat. Think of it in human terms: City officials issue smog alerts and pollen counts to warn people about possible respiratory hazards. They warn people that fish caught in local rivers or lakes may contain dangerous levels of mercury. Water is tested to determine if dangerous levels of bacteria are present. Meat is handled and cooked properly to avoid deadly bacteria. Environment affects human health…and life.

So, too, water quality in a pond affects amphibious pets.

As much as you may want to think that your backyard pond recreates nature, you can only imitate nature so far. Sparkling lakes, rivers, ponds, and streams are open systems with natural means of cleansing and replenishment. A food chain keeps the number of fish within a proper range, and the fish enjoy immensely more surface area and water volume than an artificial backyard pond can possibly hope to supply. Consider your garden pond an outdoor aquarium and seek to maintain its water quality for the health of your finned pets.

Your garden pond is more like an indoor aquarium. It is a closed system with very specific needs. Tend to its water quality for the safekeeping of aquatic pets.

Water Chemistry Basics

Water is such a common substance, we take it for granted. In setting up a garden pond, we likewise take for granted that plants adapted to growing in water and animals such as fish that naturally live within water will thrive. Pure water is composed of millions of molecules, each made up of two atoms of hydrogen joined or bound to one atom of oxygen (H_2O).

Chlorine and Chloramine

You need only consider the use of chlorine to see its potential effect in your pond. A poisonous gas, it is used to purify water and is added to most public water supplies. It kills bacteria in the water. It can harm both fish and plants. This is why aquarium keepers keep jugs of aged water, in which the chlorine has already dissipated, on hand for topping off their tanks. Fortunately, chlorine reverts easily to its natural gaseous state. It is dissipated into the air by spraying the water or by simply letting the water sit for several days. Unlike hydrogen or oxygen gases, chlorine has a detectable odor in the air.

A sure way to release chlorine from water is to use dechlorinator products. Available from pet stores, such products may be expensive if they are needed in large quantity. You can make up a stock solution of your own dechlorinator with sodium thiosulfate crystals. Dissolve 130 grams of crystals in a liter of water, or dissolve 500 grams in a gallon of water, to create a basic 14 percent solution. Store the solution in a cool, dark place. Use two drops of solution per gallon of pond volume to free the chlorine.

Many public water suppliers have discovered that chlorine can be kept within water for longer periods by supplying ammonia to bond with the chlorine to create chloramine. Both chlorine and ammonia are added to the water to effect such bonding. Spraying water into your pond does not get rid of chloramine, nor does the usual chemical dechlorination.

Chloramine's real danger to your pond life is the associated presence of ammonia. Often, chloramine-treated water straight from your tap still contains fish-toxic levels of ammonia that have not yet bonded to the chlorine gas. You can unknowingly create chloramine in your pond if you add simple chlorinated water to a pond that has ammonia in it. For example, if your water test shows the presence of ammonia and you logically decide to dilute it with a partial water exchange, the water you add contains chlorine. If you haven't gotten rid of the chlorine before it enters your pond, it will bond with the ammonia to create chloramine. That is why it is so critical that simple chlorinated water be sprayed onto the surface of your pond, to allow the chlorine gas to escape into the air before it can bind or join with ammonia, as well as before it can burn or kill your fish and plants.

You can call your public water supplier to find out if they rely on chloramines to purify your water, or you can perform an ammonia test on your tap water. If the test reflects the presence of ammonia, you are dealing with both chlorine and chloramine in your pond water. Sodium thiosulfate or dechlor products will take care of the chlorine, but you still must deal with the ammonia. In an established pond where the nitrogen cycle is fully functioning, small water additions of 5 or even 10 percent may be safely tended by the nitrifying bacteria. If you must add more than that safe percentage of pond volume at one time, treat the water for ammonia, possibly increasing your bio-filtration as well. (See Ammonia.)

pH

pH is perhaps one of the most complicated and difficult water chemistry topics to understand. It is usually defined as the measurement of free hydrogen ions in water as measured on a logarithmic scale of 1 to 14, with 7 considered neutral. A high pH reading indicates that more hydrogen ions have bonded and

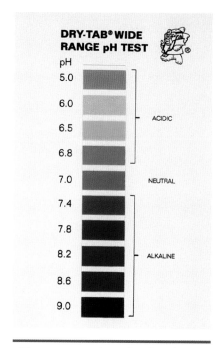

pH tests come with a color chart for comparison with the test water. Photo by Ron Everhart

are part of a molecule, primarily water molecules. Low pH readings indicate more ions in the water. Neutral is the point when the number of free hydrogen ions equals the number bound within molecules. Healthy water for your fish requires ample water molecules with oxygen, as well as a reasonable amount of free hydrogen to bind with oxygen at the surface and at aeration points such as waterfalls and venturi systems within the pond. This most healthful state of water is reflected in pH readings in the range between 5.5 and 8.5, with the neutral range of 7.0 to 7.4 considered ideal.

pH is really all about water.

Higher pH readings indicate more hydrogen within water molecules and so reflect the degree of water molecules in the pond. Oxygen is available in each molecule, supplying the needs of plants, fish, and aerobic bacteria. Low pH readings indicate a greater degree of loose hydrogen atoms or ions.

The number of free hydrogen atoms within molecules does not remain static. The water pH is in a constant state of fluctuation as oxygen is removed from water molecules, freeing hydrogen, and as hydrogen bonds with oxygen. Oxygen is removed from water molecules in several ways. Fish remove oxygen "breathing" through their gills. At night, plants take in oxygen and produce carbon dioxide, the opposite activity of daytime photosynthesis. Aerobic bacteria, ever present and the facilitators of the nitrogen cycle, use oxygen to convert ammonia into nitrite and then nitrite into nitrate. Other aerobic bacteria process organic wastes, using oxygen to fuel that activity. In all these actions, oxygen is removed from water molecules and hydrogen is set free. More free hydrogen is reflected as a lowered pH reading. It is all relative; hence, the logarithmic scale. The more loose hydrogen ions, the lower the pH reading. The less free hydrogen, the higher the pH reading.

When the water pH measures below 7.0, the neutral point, it is considered acidic. When it measures over 7.0, it is considered alkaline. Alkaline water is considered more stable chemically than acidic water since it contains more "whole" molecules with fewer stray hydrogen ions. Acidic water, possessing so many more free hydrogen ions, is susceptible to the formation of chemical bonds, and the water chemistry is altered quickly.

However, alkaline water is not safe from pH fluctuations. When plants, fish, or aerobic bacteria use oxygen in the water, their oxygen comes from the very molecules of water that are made up of two hydrogen atoms bound to one atom of oxygen. Their removal of oxygen leaves behind hydrogen atoms, as reflected by a drop in pH. Water gardens with plants measure a lower pH first thing in the morning, because the plants have removed oxygen from the water molecules during the nighttime respiration process. Too great a removal of oxygen from the water can result in a sudden drop in pH or a sudden increase in the number of free hydrogen atoms. This is known as a "pH crash." Sudden changes in pH of more than even two tenths of a point can stress fish. In a pH crash, the number of free hydrogen ions increases so rapidly that

the pH reading reflects whole integers of change. This is a deadly situation for fish that can result in perfectly healthy fish floating belly-up the next morning.

pH crashes are more likely when the water is warm and less able to hold oxygen; oxygen evaporates into the air and leaves behind free hydrogen ions. pH crashes are possible when great quantities of fish, plants, and aerobic bacteria remove oxygen from the water, leaving behind free hydrogen ions. Aerating the pond water helps prevent pH fluctuations by supplying oxygen that binds with the free hydrogen and creates more whole units of water. However, simple aeration is not enough to bind great amounts of free hydrogen and thereby bring the pH back within a desirable and stable range for your pond's life. You can stabilize the water's chemistry or prevent extreme fluctuations of the number of free hydrogen ions by providing a chemical buffering agent.

A buffer is a protective shield to ease a shock. In giving hydrogen ions a place to go, the water pH cannot swing wildly. You can increase the water's buffering capability by adding bicarbonates to the water. Bicarbonates provide ready acceptance of hydrogen ions. This capacity of the water to bind free hydrogen ions from the water, or the degree of presence of bicarbonates that perform buffering, is referred to as alkalinity. Acidic water is usually thought to require more buffering to control the number of free hydrogen ions. Yet the removal of oxygen by plants, fish, and bacteria from alkaline water creates needs, too.

If your pond water shows signs of fluctuations of more than a few tenths of a point when measured at the same time each day, you need to supply buffering to the water. Note that some fluctuation will occur during the course of any 24-hour period. Small changes are normal and are tolerated by your fish. If that fluctuation swings widely over several points, you risk stressing your fish. While goldfish and koi prefer alkaline water, they can tolerate acidic water as long as it is not turning acidic in a brief period of time. Except in the extreme ranges of the pH measure (below five and above nine), the key to fish tolerance of a pH level is the relative stability of that level.

If the water pH is lower than 5.5, your fish can experience acidosis with symptoms of anorexia, production of excess slime, isolation, and resting on the pond bottom. Untreated, their fins streak with severe stress, and they die. The condition is reversed by bringing the

pH back into a tolerable range.

If the water pH measures 8.5 or higher, fish can experience alkalosis with symptoms of excess slime coat production and gasping at the water's surface. The condition is hard to reverse and can be fatal. Alkalosis is usually encountered in concrete ponds or in heavily planted ponds where plants use up the carbon dioxide in photosynthesis, which reduces the amount of carbonic acid in the water, thereby allowing more hydrogen ions to bind into molecules, raising the water pH.

While you can change pH levels with additives such as vinegar to lower it or baking soda to raise it, the best method is to maintain a consistent, reasonable range of pH through the use of bicarbonates that buffer the water. Use crushed oyster shell, crushed limestone, or SeaChem Neutral Regulator. In an emergency or a pH crash, add 1 teaspoon of baking soda per 5–10 gallons of water. Check the pH an hour later to be sure it has risen.

Because so many factors can affect your pond's pH, testing it should be part of your weekly water testing. If a fish appears troubled, include pH monitoring with your tests for ammonia and nitrite. If your pond contains a heavy bioload—including fish, plants, decomposing organic matter, and aerobic bacterial action in a

bio-filter—you can assist in preventing sudden drops of pH by providing ample aeration.

The Nitrogen Cycle

Whether or not you supply bio-filtration to your pond, and even if you do not have fish in your pond, the nitrogen cycle can occur. All it needs is the presence of organic matter. The decomposition of organic matter by aerobic or oxygen-using bacteria generates the waste product ammonia. Ammonia waste is also produced by fish. As soon as you have ammonia present in the water, the nitrogen cycle becomes a major player in the state of your water chemistry.

Aerobic bacteria, *Nitrosomonas*, use oxygen on the ammonia and produce a by-product, nitrite. Another aerobic bacteria, *Nitrobacter*, then works on the nitrite and produces the final by-product in the cycle, nitrate. Even a small quantity of ammonia is toxic to fish and can burn their gills and stress them. Nitrite is toxic to fish. It prevents their blood from carrying oxygen. In the presence of phosphates, nitrate is food for plants.

The nitrogen cycle takes four to six weeks to establish. Its cycling presence is indicated in water testing by an initial measure of ammonia followed a

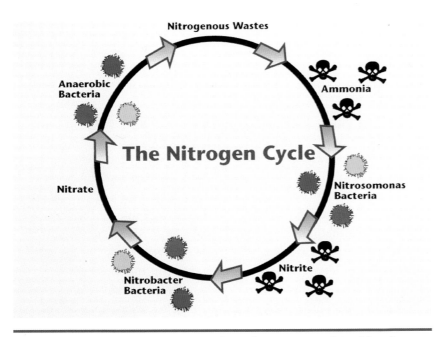

The nitrogen cycle. Drawing courtesy of Chic Kelty, International Pond Supplies

few weeks later by a measure of nitrite, followed a few weeks later by the tested presence of nitrate. Once the cycle is functioning, sufficient quantities of nitrifying bacteria ensure that wastes in the pond are safely processed.

In the warm-climate pond, where water temperatures do not dip below 55°F, the nitrogen cycle occurs year-round. In the temperate pond, where water temperatures go below 55°F, the nitrogen cycle and the workings of nitrifying bacteria are temperature-dependent. The bacteria are dormant below 55°F. When the water warms above 55°F, they awaken and participate in the cycle again. The implication of this temperature-dependency is that during the winter your water may test pos-

itive for the presence of ammonia produced by your lethargic fish, but it will not test positive for any nitrite presence. As the pond warms in the spring, your testing will reflect the initial presence of ammonia generated by your fish, followed by a tested presence of nitrite, and finally by a tested presence of nitrate as the cycle assumes regular activity. In the great bodies of water in nature, the nitrogen cycle can easily accommodate ammonia wastes. In our backyard ponds, however, which are often maxed out on bio-loading of fish and other organic presences, naturally occurring nitrifying bacteria may not be present in sufficiently large number to cycle ammonia wastes safely. Extra bacteria may be needed to do the job.

Bio-filters that provide more homes for the colonizing aerobic bacteria are used. A continued positive test for ammonia or nitrite beyond the initial start-up peaks indicates a need for additional bio-filtration or a reduction in the bio-load, i.e., find homes for your extra fish.

Ammonia

Ammonia, the primary waste product of fish, is excreted primarily through gill tissue, but also through the kidneys. It also occurs from aerobically decomposing organic matter such as plant tissue and fish feces. Ammonia accumulations cause reddening of the skin and damage to the sensitive gills of the fish. Signs of ammonia stress include fish isolating themselves, lying on the pond bottom, holding their fins tightly clamped to their bodies, and excess slime coat production. Even minute amounts of ammonia depress the immune system of fish and make fish more susceptible to pests and disease. Any measurable ammonia present in your pond water is not tolerable.

Ammonia presence is usually due to the presence of too many fish or to your feeding the fish too much. It can also be due to ammonia that is added to your water supply to create the longer-lived chloramine. When the water pH registers higher than 8.0, most of the ammonia present deionizes to fish-toxic levels. Ammonia in water that exists in its nontoxic ionized form of ammonium tests below 7.4 pH. This means that water testing below 7.4 allows the ammonia molecule, which has one atom of nitrogen and three of hydrogen, to snap in an extra hydrogen ion to make a molecule containing one atom of nitrogen and four of hydrogen. With higher pH readings, there are fewer free hydrogen atoms. Above 8.0, there is simply not enough available to detoxify the NH_3 ammonia.

At the first indication of ammonia presence, begin daily water changes of 20 to 40 percent of the pond's volume. So long as your testing continues to reflect ammonia presence, cut back on the amount of food given your fish. Check the pH to determine if you need to buffer the water.

Aquarium chemists and pond supply manufacturers offer products that convert the NH_3 toxic form of ammonia into nontoxic NH_4 ammonium. The process is referred to as "binding." In this case, binding involves adding the extra hydrogen atom to the ammonia molecule that already has three hydrogen atoms. As soon as the fourth hydrogen atom joins the molecule, the molecule is changed into a slightly different form, nontoxic ammonium. These products use sodium hydroxymethane sulfinate or di-hydroxymethane to make this nontoxic form of ammonia. None of these products removes ammonia from the water; they simply alter the ammonia chemically into its nontoxic form. However, because typical ammonia tests do not differentiate between the two forms of ammonia, you cannot tell if the toxic form of ammonia has been removed. The water continues to test positive for ammonia. There is an ammonia test kit for both the NH_3 and NH_4, but it is not commonly available. A fairly simple way to figure that the nontoxic ammonium form has been achieved is to test the pH of the water. If it is below 7.4, the ammonia is probably ionized.

Another way to rid your water of fish-toxic ammonia is to physically remove the ammonia. This is accomplished with zeolite, a soft, white mineral that is commonly used in aquarium filtration systems. Zeolite absorbs ammonia, taking the ammonia and bonding it to its own molecules. (This is as compared to *adsorption*, which accumulates substances on the surface, and which is performed by carbon within the aquarium filter.) After two or three weeks, the zeolite will have absorbed as much ammonia as it is capable of bonding, and you will notice a tested presence of ammonia again. You can make the zeolite release its store of ammonia by soaking it in a solution of one pound of salt dissolved in five gallons of water. The salt removes the ammonia with a chemical bonding, leaving the zeolite free to absorb more ammonia. The zeolite can then be returned to the pond water to remove more ammonia.

Knowing that you can cause zeolite to release its store of ammonia in salt water explains why you should not make the mistake of using salt as a fish treatment when zeolite is present. Your salt treatment can end up releasing stress-producing or toxic ammonia into your pond.

Nitrite

Unlike ammonia, which is produced directly in the water as a fish waste, nitrite occurs as a by-product of the nitrogen cycle. It is even more deadly, because it suppresses the ability of a fish to carry oxygen in its bloodstream, resulting in what is commonly known as "brown blood disease." Even a slight presence of nitrogen stresses fish. Larger amounts cause suffocation and death. Besides the stress-produced blushing and red-veining on the fish's body, such an afflicted fish will display widely flared gills as its body tries vainly to acquire more oxygen.

Your pond water will test positive for nitrite during the initial start-up phase of your bio-filter. It will test positive for nitrite at other times if too many fish are in the pond or if your bio-filter is not big enough to tend to the needs of the pond.

No product will physically remove nitrite from water. You can only dilute it, remove the affected water totally, or, if you have the luxury of time, establish the nitrogen cycle with *Nitrobacter* bacteria converting the toxic nitrite into nitrate. Once the presence of nitrite is felt within your pond, its toxicity to your fish requires immediate action. You can't wait a few weeks or even a few days for the *Nitrobacter* to kick in.

To combat nitrite, dissolve one teaspoon of non-iodized salt per gallon of pond water and add it all at once in conjunction with up to a 40 percent daily water exchange. Methylene Blue may help the fish somewhat with the nitrite poisoning, but it will not fully reverse the condition. A fish displaying only fin and tail blushing is usually saved with prompt remedial action. A fish displaying red body veining may be too far gone to be saved. Moving these fish into fresh, nitrite-free and salt-treated water may provide them with their only chance of survival.

Nitrate

Nitrate is usually of no concern to the pondkeeper if plants are present in the pond. In the presence of phosphates, nitrates are plant food. Without the presence of plants, however, nitrates can accumulate and cause sickness in fish, evidenced by bloody fins and weakness that leaves them susceptible to parasites and disease. Because koi ponds often do not include plants, nitrate problems tend to affect koi more than goldfish.

In the planted pond, high nitrate presence is indicated by blue-green algae, a foul-smelling bluish algae that grows on the underside of lily pads. When nitrates measure over 100mg/l, you may notice slowed growth in your smaller fish. Many of the little ones may die off for no apparent reason. Occasionally, blushing in the fins and tail may also be noticed

Plants, such as these water hyacinth, are highly effective at removing nitrates from pond water.

in smaller fish. Although koi rarely display symptoms of excess nitrates in the water, a goldfish may list to one side and hang motionless in the water.

Water hyacinth and *Elodea canadensis* are among the most

directly from the water. If your pond does not offer plants and nitrates are causing problems for your fish, perform daily water changes of up to forty percent of the pond's volume, remembering to treat the water

that work within the nitrogen cycle need oxygen. Fortunately, water is made up of molecules of H_2O, two atoms of hydrogen bound to one atom of oxygen. This is the oxygen source for the lives within your pond.

Your fish will tell you if the oxygen levels are low, gasping at the water's surface or gathering near water entry points in your pond. Because plants use oxygen during the nighttime hours in their respiration, you may notice your fish gasping at the surface in the very early morning hours. Green-water algae, as a single-celled plant, can also depress oxygen levels overnight. The immediate remedy is to supply additional aeration to the pond water.

Gasping at the water's surface may indicate your fish need oxygen, not food.

efficient removers of nitrate from the system. Use floating plants in the top of your bio-filter or add them directly to the pond. koi pond keepers can use floating plants in the pond if they are rotated with others from a separate tub as the koi nibble away roots, or by providing the plants with protective netting. Plants potted in soil can be planted in soilless media or in lava rock to allow their roots to seek the nitrate

addition/pond for chlorine, until the water tests with less than 20mg/l of nitrate presence. In any event, it is likely you have too many fish in the pond; consider digging another pond.

Dissolved Oxygen

Dissolved oxygen is critical to a healthy pond. Your fish need oxygen. Your plants need oxygen. And aerobic bacteria

Warm water holds less oxygen than cooler water, as heat weakens the bond between the hydrogen atoms and the oxygen atom in each molecule, releasing the oxygen to the air (and leaving the orphaned hydrogen atoms behind). In its most obvious case, heating water to boiling, you see steam rising from the water. So long as your pond water temperature is under 86°F, enough oxygen remains in the water to still allow normal feeding of your fish. Because they use more oxygen in digesting their food, you should temporarily stop feeding them in water warmer than 86°F when oxygen presence is depressed. A partial water exchange may be needed to lower the water's temperature and ease the oxygen deficiency.

A relatively inexpensive test kit for oxygen is available from pet stores. Like the liquid test

pump and stone, use a venturi apparatus to inject additional air into the water, or, as a quick-fix, temporary solution, use hydrogen peroxide. Working only as long as four hours, use one-half cup of

gency measure as you remedy the problem with additional aeration. As with most other water-quality considerations, the amount of fish (and plants) in your pond directly impacts the amount of oxygen in the water. Acidic water, too, may also have low oxygen levels.

Testing Your Pond Water

Whenever your fish or plants appear distressed, immediately test the water. Test kits for ammonia, nitrite, nitrate, and pH are readily available at pet stores. If the water temperature is less than sixty degrees, collect your water sample and bring it indoors to warm up to room temperature before performing the test.

During the early part of the pond season, you should closely monitor your pond's chemistry, especially if your fish load is near your pond's maximum load or if the water experiences an algae bloom. Once the nitrogen cycle has established, testing can be performed weekly or bi-weekly.

Supplemental aeration to your pond can be supplied by a waterfall, spouting ornaments, and bubbling fountains set within the water.

kits, it involves comparing a water sample to a color chart. The minimum oxygen level for fish to survive for a few days is 5 ppm. If the readings are as low as 3 ppm, your fish will be belly-up in no time. You should strive to have your oxygen levels testing from 8 to 14 ppm for your fish's best health. Even levels as low as 7 might be supplemented with mechanical aeration.

To increase oxygen, provide additional aeration with an air-

hydrogen peroxide per one hundred gallons of pond water. Since applying it directly or near your fish can cause gill damage, dilute the hydrogen peroxide in a container of water before adding it to the pond. Some fish keepers prefer to squirt the hydrogen peroxide directly into the water, being careful not to direct the spray near fish. Because hydrogen peroxide works for such a short period, consider it an emer-

Water Changes

Water changes may be part of your regular pond maintenance or they may be required as remedies to water-quality problems occurring within the pond. Observe the following precautions:

1. Use a dechlorinator in water changes of more than 5 to 10 percent of the total volume of the pond.
2. Be sure the water being added is close to the existing temperature of the pond water.
3. Be sure the water you are adding is within a safe (.2) pH range of the existing pond water.
4. Use the total-alkalinity test to be sure extensive water change does not result in electrolyte-poor water.

If plants are not present in the pond, a teaspoon of non-iodized salt per gallon of water in a major water change helps ease fish stress. (See Salt, Chapter 5.) Be sure the pond is not being serviced by zeolite if you are using salt in the water.

Water Temperature

Temperature is very important to the capability of water to hold oxygen. Water in excess of 86°F becomes depressed in oxygen capability and requires a remedy.

Gradually cooling water allows a fish to produce cold-water enzymes in its protective slime coat. Sudden drops in temperature can stress and kill fish. This is the rationale behind the humane method of fish euthanasia of placing a fish in a plastic bag filled with water and putting the bag in the freezer.

Probably the most critical of temperature-influenced factors is the temperature of 60°F. When the water temperature drops below 60°, the immune system of the fish begins to shut down. By the time the temperature has lowered to 50°F, your fish is unable to fight off parasites and disease. Usually these critical periods occur in the autumn and spring. Problems arise in this 10-degree range because parasites and disease-bearing bacteria remain active. One way to protect your fish from this treacherous temperature range is to heat the pond water. If you can provide enough heat to the water to maintain a temperature of about 62°F, fine. If this proves to be impractical, your fish are better off in unfreezing temperatures below 40°F, in which both parasites and bacteria are dormant. Using salt at a three percent solution during these cold-water times gives further protection to your fish, especially from the more cold-tolerant *Costia*. (See Fish Health, Chapter 5.)

Hydrogen Sulfide (H₂S)

Hydrogen sulfide is toxic to fish. We learned this lesson the hard way, not once, but twice—once in an indoor aquarium and once outside, in a huge, lined, 100×50-foot pond. In the 55-gallon aquarium, it took a year for the hydrogen sulfide to become an issue. Outdoors, it took 10 years. The results were the same: all fish dead.

Hydrogen sulfide is the by-product of anaerobic bacteria that decompose organic matter within a layer of sediment that builds up on the pond bottom, within sand, gravel, or stone on the bottom of the system, or within a layer of sediment that accumulates in your filtration system. This is not the same bacteria that work aerobically on the surface of dead organic matter. Those bacteria use oxygen from the surrounding water to produce a by-product of ammonia. Anaerobic bacteria use sulfur instead of oxygen in their metabolic process. Their by-product is hydrogen sulfide. While there is a test kit for its presence, you can infer its presence if you have a layer of gravel or rocks in your pond bottom, or if you can actually see the mulm buildup on the pond bottom or within your filter. Disturbing the substrate produces the telltale smell of rotten eggs. Only recently I talked with a landscaper/pond installer who noted that in only its second year, his backyard pond, which is covered with a layer of gravel and rocks on the bottom, is beginning to smell. One can only hope his fish are not named.

In the presence of hydrogen sulfide, the only solution is to remove all fish immediately to safe waters and fully drain and clean the pond. Even this may not save the fish. Do not attempt to clean the offending gravel with the fish still in such a dirty pond; you will release even more hydrogen sulfide in the process and probably kill any remaining fish.

Potassium permanganate can be used to degrade hydrogen sulfide if applied at 1–2 ppm (1/4 to 1/2 gram per 100 gallons). At this strength, hydrogen sulfide is reduced to nontoxic compounds and even the offending detritus that is feeding the anaerobic bacteria is oxidized. However, as a caustic compound, potassium permanganate can kill your fish and plants if not used appropriately, as well as present a risk to your own health. If your pond has a gravel bottom and requires this treatment, you may decide to remove fish and plants to safe quarters for this extreme remedy. Be sure to disconnect your bio-filter; potassium permanganate will kill your beneficial bacteria, too. To treat water for hydrogen sulfide presence, potassium permanganate should never be used at a strength beyond the pink color, yet the pink color must be maintained for a full 10 to 12 hours. If the water starts to turn brownish in less than 10–12 hours, the organics in the pond have removed the energy of the chemical, and you need to re-dose. Continue re-dosing until the water remains its initial pink for the full 10–12 hours. You will then fully empty the pond and remove as much of the oxidized material as you can. Refill the pond with fresh water and attend to the pond as a new setup. As you can see, this is a lengthy, messy, and risky process. To those gardeners who long for the natural look of a rock-lined pond, yes, you can install such a feature…but be prepared to clean the rocks extensively of the hidden buildup of sediment that contributes to anaerobic bacterial activity and the resulting hydrogen sulfide toxicity. (See potassium permanganate, Chapter 5.)

Algae Control

Most people consider algae aesthetically. Green-water algae make water murky, making it difficult to see and enjoy fish. Filamentous or string algae look slimy and detract from the

Covering the bottom of your pond with rocks allows organic matter to collect unseen. The anaerobic bacteria that consume the hidden mulm produce hydrogen sulfide, a foul-smelling, fish-toxic gas.

beauty of the pond. A little bit of algae, especially the mossy algae that grows on pond walls and pot sides, function like submerged aquatic plants in the pond, helping to remove nitrates from the water. This type of algae actually naturalizes the pond construction, camouflaging the liner and giving the pond an established look.

Keep in mind that algae are plants. As plants, they require sunlight and nitrates for the process of photosynthesis during the daylight hours. At night they require oxygen for respiration. As plants, they can create problems far more serious to your fish than aesthetics. An excess of algae in the pond, especially single-cell, green-water algae, can create critical oxygen shortages within the water. Your fish will let you know by gasping at the water surface early in the morning. This same oxygen-depletion by the algae also impacts the water pH, breaking down water molecules to use the oxygen and leaving free hydrogen ions loose in the water. The resulting swing in the pH from its normal range during the day to the drastically lowered level occurring overnight can present critical stress to your fish.

An occasional algae bloom in the pond is normal, especially in the early spring before plants are able to take nitrate from the water sufficiently. Patience, along with watching the fish for signs of oxygen needs, usually gets you through this short period. When algae do not clear up with the aid of growing plants, however, it is time to take action before problems with oxygen and pH occur.

A persistent algae problem usually indicates excess nutrient

Prolonged green-water episodes are more than unsightly. They also affect the oxygen and pH levels in your pond.

production in the pond. The guilty parties? Your fish. Check your fish number and see about making the load in the pond lighter.

As long as the pond is not seriously overloaded with fish, you have some remedies available.

You can take the easy way out and use a UV light on single-celled plants. This also provides a mechanical means of filtering dead algae from the pond, preventing them from adding to the nutrient load and contributing to even more algae growth. UV control of algae is becoming *de rigueur* in koi keeping.

Supplying enough plants to compete effectively with the algae for available nutrients is a proven solution. Water hyacinths and the submerged plants *Elodea canadensis* and *Ceratophyllum demersum* (hornwort or coontail) are especially effective plants to use. We like the *Elodea canadensis* because in our zone 5 climate it breaks dormancy a good two weeks before other plants. The result: no algae blooms at all! As long as your fish load in the pond is reasonable, one bunch of submerged plants per square foot of water surface prevents algae blooms. Plant control of algae is effective in the goldfish/water garden. It can also be used in koi ponds that include plants, whether within the pond itself, within a separate but connected pond, or within the tops of bio-filters. Water hyacinths are especially effective in bio-filters.

Another method that works is to attack the algae by depriving them of light. Water dyes, usually blue or black, are available to shade the water and prevent sunlight from entering and fostering algae growth. Many botanic gardens resort to this remedy. These dyes are especially effective at controlling filamentous or string algae. Their primary drawback is that they color the water. You can still see your fish when they are near the surface, but their colors are distorted. Because this defeats the purpose of selecting particular koi, using dyes is not a preferred method of control in the koi pond. In the goldfish/water garden, move your submerged aquatic plants close to the water surface, at least initially, to ensure them enough sunlight to grow.

Two remedies in the marketplace are not advisable for ponds with fish.

Flocculants that cause algae cells to clump together for easier removal either by mechanical filtration or by a fine-mesh swimming pool skimmer net may also cause obstruction to fish gills and may disturb the dissolved oxygen levels in the pond.

Chemicals such as copper sulfate or Simazine do kill algae...along with other pond plants. Even if you remove your pond plants to a separate tank, you may still risk fish health by using these chemicals. Copper products cause fish to lose the protective slime coat that protects their immune system. Simazine is reputedly safe for use with fish, but it can result in serious health problems for your fish. Ponds without plants, such as koi ponds, that use Simazine to control algae may experience buildups of nitrate, the end product of the nitrogen cycle in bio-filtration. Excess nitrate can cause red mouth lesions and lethargy in koi.

Pond Filtration

As soon as you hook up a recirculating pump in your pond, you must deal with filtration. Mechanical filtration prevents the circulation of particulate matter that might stress the pump and burn it up. Bio-filtration—the enhancement of the naturally occurring nitrogen cycle in the water—becomes important in the pond maximally stocked with fish or at its bio-load capacity. The type of filtration you use depends entirely on the bio-load of the pond, and, to a lesser degree, on your budget.

As soon as you add fish and a circulating pump to your pond, filtration becomes a concern.

You can increase the mechanical filtration of submersible pumps by wrapping the pump in foam and enclosing it within a basket for easy retrieval from the water for cleaning as necessary.

Mechanical Filtration

Most submersible pumps come equipped with a mesh screen between the pond water and the intake outlet of the pump. This prevents sediment from circulating through the pump. Because sediment naturally occurs on the pond bottom, you should set up your pump an inch or so above the bottom of the pond. You can prop up the pump on a brick, for example, to elevate it above the sediment. Regularly check the screen on the pump to ensure that it is not becoming so clogged as to decrease the water flow through the pump. A decrease in the water flow through your waterfall or spouting ornaments will let you know that the screen needs to be hosed clean. Because this is part of the regular maintenance of your submersible pump, you may wish to set up your pump within a mesh basket to make its retrieval from the water easier. Using such a basket also allows you to provide more mechanical filtration as you fill the basket around the pump with reticulated foam or lava rock. Pumps that offer attachments for such filtration may float to the surface when they become too dirty, or the attachment may come free of the pump. Regular cleaning of the mechanical filter assures optimum function.

Additional mechanical filtration apart from the pump may also be desirable, particularly if the pond has many plants or fish. You know you need more mechanical filtration if you can see particulates in suspension within the water. This additional mechanical filtration may be nothing more than a reservoir containing additional media of reticulated foam or lava rock through which the water flows before returning to the pond via a waterfall. Bio-filtration will occur in such setups. Therefore, it is important to clean the media regularly to prevent the aerobic bacteria from suffocating because of sediment buildup. If you must clean the media more than once every two weeks, you need more mechanical filtration.

Vegetable Filtration

Vegetable filtration, or the use of plants to remove particulates and dissolved nutrients in the water, is appropriate for the pond lightly stocked with fish. While you can use a small reservoir set at the head of the waterfall return of recycling water, a stream design is especially effective, as is a separate vegetable pond. The general formula is to have your vegetable filter equal at least 10 percent of the volume of the pond it serves.

For a very small pond three or four feet wide, a whiskey barrel-size container can serve as a vegetable filter. Simply install the container at the top of your waterfall and fill it with water hyacinths, water celery, or a combination of floating and marginal aquatic plants. Constructing a dual pond system with the upper pond devoted to growing submerged aquatics or water hyacinths for maximum nutrient removal, along with marginal aquatic plants and even a water lily or two, expands the size of a pond you can filter vegetatively.

STREAM VEGETABLE FILTERS

Unlike on the stagnant pond bottom, gravel can be used in the stream bed since the flowing water allows the aerobic sludge-eating bacteria to

Vegetable filtration can be supplied with plants such as water celery (Oenanthe) set up to grow hydroponically in a flow-through chamber.

tend to any solid wastes not used by the plants grown directly in the bed. Keeping the movement through the stream at a gentle flow allows nitrifying bacteria to colonize the gravel bed and provide bio-filtration, too. Side pockets allow growing space for submerged aquatics or water hyacinths.

Be careful plants do not grow to fill the bed and raise the water level in the stream to the height of the hidden liner. Without monitoring and pruning the plant growth, you can end up with water loss. During autumn, erect a netting over the length of the stream to prevent clogging, flooding, and water-quality deterioration from fallen leaves.

PLANTS TO GROW IN STREAMS

Maximum benefit is derived from planting directly into the gravel base of the system. Especially vigorous plants are marked with an asterisk; they require judicious monitoring/pruning to prevent the stream from flooding. Naturally, these are the most effective plants in vegetable filtration.

Acorus calamus, Sweetflag
Acorus gramineus, Dwarf sweetflag
Butomus umbellatus, Flowering rush
Calla palustris, Bog arum
Caltha palustris, Marsh marigold
Cardamine cordifolia, Heartleaved bittercress*

*Craig Luna of Atlanta, Georgia, frequently plants dwarf variegated sweet flag (*Acorus gramineus* 'Variegata') directly into the stream bed to help remove nutrients from the water, at the same time enhancing the stream design.*

Carex obnupta, Slough hedge
Cyperus alternifolius, Umbrella palm
Echinodorus cordifolia, Radican sword
Eleocharis palustris, Common spike rush
Eriophorum angustifolium, Cotton grass
Houttuynia cordata*
Hydrocotyle umbellata, Pennywort*
Iris ensata, Japanese iris
Iris fulva, Red water iris
Iris laevigata
Iris pseudacorus, Yellow flag iris
Iris versicolor, Blue flag iris
Juncus spp., Rush
Lysimmachia nummularia,

Creeping Jenny*
Menyanthes trifoliata, Bog bean
Mimulus spp., Monkey flower
Myriophyllus aquaticum, Parrot's feather*
Nasturtium officinale, Watercress*
Oenanthe, Water celery*
Peltandra virginica, Spoonflower
Pontederia cordata, Pickerel weed
Ranunculus flammula, Small creeping spearwort*
Sagittaria spp., Arrowhead
Saururus cernuus, Lizard tail
Scirpus spp., Rush
Typha spp., Cattail*

Surface-Skimming Filtration

In the early 1980s, Joe B. Dekker introduced a version of the swimming pool skimmer system that he developed for use in garden ponds. Since then, several companies have devised manufactured adaptations of that system. The design involves installing a small container adjacent to the pond wall. The container allows water to enter from the pond. Inside the container is a mesh laundry bag that collects surface debris from the pond. The submersible pump sits in the bottom of the unit. Plumbing directs the water to the top of the waterfall system where a small bio-filter unit may be installed.

These systems are very effective for the pond sited where leaf fall is a year-round problem. You should, however, provide solutions to two problems with the system. Provide a mesh barrier grate between the pump and the rest of the container area to prevent small fish and frogs from being drawn into the pump or up against the intake screen and killed. This grate should separate the entire bottom of the unit containing the pump from the rest of the container, so small fish are not subject to the pull of the water to the pump inlet.

The second problem to be solved is even more critical. Ponds that rely solely on a surface-skimmer system for water recycling circulate only the top layer of water in the pond. Since the primary access to dissolved oxygen is at the surface, where water touches air, these systems cycle only the most oxygen-rich waters in the pond. The water in the deepest parts of the pond remains stagnant and unaerated. Ponds maximally stocked with fish, ponds with green-water algae, and ponds with warmer water can experience serious oxygen deficiency that jeopardizes the fish. If you use such a system, be sure to use a second pump on the pond bottom or a bottom-drain circulating system to cycle and aerate those "dead" waters.

A skimmer filtration system, hidden beneath the flat rock in the foreground, can be beneficial to the pond sited near constantly falling leaves. You will still need to address the problem of baby fish being trapped and killed within the system and the critical problem of stagnant and low-oxygenated water within the pond.

The very small pond can be served by a whiskey barrel-size bio-filter set in the top of the waterfall return.

Bio-Filtration

Bio-filtration involves supplying media for colonizing by the nitrifying bacteria that convert ammonia into nitrite and nitrite into nitrate. Plan your bio-filter for 10 to 20 percent of the pond volume. Remember that the bacteria at work in your bio-filter are aerobic. They do not work where they do not touch the oxygenated water flowing past them. Allowing sediment to collect on the bio-filter media decreases the effectiveness of the bacteria or may even suffocate them. Such sedimentary collection also invites the activity of anaerobic bacteria, which produce toxic hydrogen sulfide. You should

also supply adequate mechanical filtration to any water flowing through your bio-filter.

Various media will work in your bio-filter. As a general rule, avoid sand and small gravels that compact easily, as they soon deteriorate into a channeling action, and the water will flow through only a very limited portion of the media. Lava rock is still considered a very effective media because it offers considerable surface area for colonizing bacteria. Its primary drawback is the weight of any quantity of the media. Many people have found that bagging the media inside mesh onion bags makes for easy removal and cleaning. Newer options are narrow,

plastic ribbon known as bio-ribbon and small plastic balls of various shapes known as bio-balls. Both of these are lightweight, long-lived, and effective media.

It is important that water flows through your bio-filter to offer the aerobic bacteria a continual source of oxygen. The water should flow slowly enough to allow them to do their job, one to two gallons per minute, or 60 to 120 gallons per hour per square foot of media surface area.

In recent years, high efficiency bio-filter systems have been developed for the larger ponds typically used by koi keepers. These systems are out-of-pond, involving designs such

Bio-Filter

Media

Options

Lava rock remains a favorite medium of goldfish keepers. It needs to be removed for cleaning. Photo courtesy of Maryland Aquatic Nurseries

A newer option is volcanic rock media, smaller and lighter than lava rock. This medium is so light, it can be stirred within its chamber for backwash cleaning.

One of the larger versions of bio-balls, a plastic fabrication that offers ample surface area for bacteria and a long life for your pocketbook.

Bio-ribbon, made of thin plastic ribbon, has become a popular, long-lived medium. Shown above the bio-ribbon is a layer of plastic foam that prevents particulate matter from hampering the work of the bacteria.

A smaller, more recently developed version of the bio-ball media presents extensive surface area and long life.

Because of the larger size of koi, and because of koi keepers' obsession with the incredible breed, bio-filtration is a necessary part of the koi pond.

as the bubble-bead and fluid-bed systems and the three- or four-chamber vortex system.

BIO-FILTRATION FOR GOLDFISH AND TURTLE PONDS

Goldfish and turtle ponds are usually well served by easily constructed bio-filtration systems. Usually these systems rely on a gravity return and are sited at the top of the system in the initial waterfall entry channel. A 3 × 5-foot pond can be served by a whiskey barrel-size container. Larger ponds are better served by heavy-duty rubber, horse-trough–type containers. Water is pumped by a submersible pump through a flexible pipe to the entry point at the top of the waterfall where it flows through the system and back into the pond. The two most effective designs are the up-flow and the horizontal-flow.

In an up-flow system, the pump sends water to the top of the filter, where it flows down a PVC pipe to the bottom of the unit. With a grate fitted several inches above the bottom of the container, solid wastes go into an open cavity before the water flows upward through the filter media—lava rock, bio-ribbon, or bio-balls—to exit through a port into the waterfall system. The collected solid wastes are emptied through the bottom drain. A cone-shaped vat is especially easy to maintain and offers a deeper point for the

The Living Pond

wastes to exit. This style filter allows for backwashing or injecting a strong jet of water into the bottom to clean it.

Horizontal-flow systems pump the water through a side wall of the filter unit to flow horizontally through the media and then exit through a port on the opposite side. Often, these systems include baffling walls of reticulated foam or suspended brushes to create a zigzag flow of the water through the system. This allows particulate matter to settle out. If the water is moving slowly enough, the solid matter drops to the bottom of the system where it can be flushed away via a bottom drain. Cleaning these systems involves draining them, removing the media, and hosing the media separately from the unit.

BIO-FILTRATION FOR KOI PONDS

Any pond maintaining a maximum bio-load needs bio-filtration. Because koi ponds tend to be larger in surface area, and contain a greater volume of water, they require elaborate systems. Because koi grow so large and because koi keepers cannot seem to resist adding just one more, an adequate-size bio-filter is critical to the healthy survival of these special pets.

Whatever style of bio-filter is used, begin with a bottom

drain. If it is set up to pull solids constantly from the pond bottom as the water recycles, it avoids unhealthy conditions and problems associated with collected wastes. Swimming pool type skimmers are also used to remove debris from the surface before the debris settles at the pond bottom. Submersible pumps are not usually used with larger koi ponds since the pumping capacity required is greater than that supplied by most lines of submersibles. Sump pumps are available to pump such volumes, but the cost of running them is significant in comparison to the energy consumed by more efficient out-of-pond, mag-drive pumps. The two primary systems in use today are bubble-bead filters/fluid-bed filters and the vortex system.

Bubble-Bead and Fluid-Bed Filters

Bubble-bead filters are also known as buoyant-bead filters. Based on an up-flow design, water is pumped into the bottom of the large filter chamber in which tiny beads are suspended. The beads float to the top of the chamber and compress slightly to create a bio-mechanical filter bed. Particulate matter is collected among them, even as colonizing bacteria tend to the reduction of ammonia and nitrites. Only one percent of the pond volume

A bubble-bead filter is best hidden away near the pond.

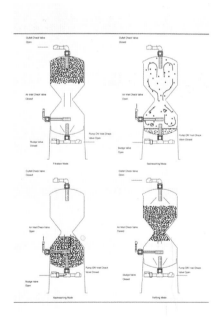

Diagram of bubble-bead filter operation
Drawing courtesy of Chic Kelty, International Pond Supplies

needs to be involved in this system to effect biological balance of the pond's water, even in the face of considerable fish loading.

Set at some distance from the pond, where it may be camouflaged by fencing structures or landscaping, the bubble-bead filter must be backwashed each day. The pump is turned off and the bottom drain is opened. As water leaves the chamber, air is drawn inside, with its air bubbles agitating the bead media and dislodging particulates to be discharged from the bottom. The pump is then turned on again to resume normal operation. The larger models that are designed for ponds of 20,000 or more gallons come equipped with a built-in, motorized cleaning system.

Similar to the bubble-bead systems, fluid-bed filters use a smaller bead to effect an even greater "polishing" of the water. They, too, require backwashing to flush wastes from the system. Unless you can be available at least once a week and as much as almost daily to maintain the system, it is worth the extra money to install the self-cleaning enhancement.

Both systems require a high-pressure–tolerant pump, much like those used to operate swimming pool filtration systems. Recent developments are producing more energy-efficient pumps that ease much

A demonstration model of the fluid-bed filter displays the suspended action of the small media particles inside.

of the former costs of operation.

When this technology was first introduced, many koi keepers were dismayed at the presence of green water in their ponds. It was soon determined that the use of an ultraviolet light in conjunction with the system fully eradicated the problem. (See koi Pond Construction.)

Vortex System

The vortex system is an adaptation of the old-fashioned, tried-and-true chamber system of filtration. Water first enters a vortex chamber. Because it enters the chamber below the water level, it causes the water to rotate, spinning the heavier solid particles to the chamber's

bottom. A plug at the bottom of the cone-shaped vat allows the solids to be purged from the system. A small grate over the purge area allows larger debris to be collected.

Water leaves the vortex chamber through a side port and enters the next vat, which is filled with mechanical filtration media such as reticulated foam mats of various porosity. This further removes particulate matter from the water.

Flowing horizontally, water moves through an opposite port and into the next vat-chamber, where bio-media is supplied for the active colonies of nitrifying bacteria. This media may be bio-ribbon, bio-balls, or a coarsely graded volcanic ash material of light weight and ample surface area. Many large koi ponds include a fourth chamber containing more bio-media. The water is then directed past a UV light and back into the system to return by way of the waterfall.

The real beauty of the vortex system is that maintenance is reduced to purging the settling chamber perhaps once every week or two, depending on the pond's bio-load. It can be installed at some distance from the pond, perhaps housed within a shed or garage, tucked around the corner of the house, or hidden behind landscaping. The cone-shaped vats are available in small to very large sizes

The first chamber of the three or four used in the vortex system is a chamber that settles particulate matter from the water before it flows horizontally into the next chamber for bio-filtration.

Pond designer Beau Roye of Dallas, Texas, demonstrates the extent of preformed sizes of vortex chambers to suit koi pond needs.

and can accommodate even large koi ponds. The critical point of their installation is that the water level within the vats be level with the water within the pond. Plumbing from the pond to the system ideally should not include elbows; if it does, the elbows should be carefully flushed free of trapped air pockets. Air is less likely if the elbows do not extend above the water level.

WINTERIZING YOUR BIO-FILTER AND JUMP-STARTING IT FOR SPRING

From Suburban Water Gardens' Bob BonGiorno, in Dix Hills, New York, comes a helpful tip for winterizing your bio-filter and using this year's bio-filter to jump-start next year's.

Once the water temperatures have stabilized below 50°F, remove the bio-media from your bio-filter and gently clean it with pond water pumped through your pump. Although the bacterial colony is barely functioning, bacteria go into hibernation in cold but not freezing water. As long as they have not frozen, they are still alive. Too strong a hosing can wash away the bacterial colony. Clean the rest of the bio-filter with a strong hosing.

The cleaned bio-media with its colony of sluggish aerobic bacteria is used to create what Bob calls a "jump-start soup." You will need to maintain your bacterial starter at 65°F. If you cannot keep the setup in such a warm place, use a thermostatically controlled aquarium heater. Because these bacteria are aerobic, supply oxygen with an aquarium air pump and air stone placed in the bottom of the starter container.

Place the bio-media into a clean container or garbage pail equipped with the heater, if necessary. Fill the container with enough water to cover the media and set up the aerator device. To help control evaporation and keep the media clean, cover the container. Drill a hole in the lid for the air tubing to prevent the cover from crimping it. Set a thermometer in the water to be sure it remains at the desired 65°F. Start with a few drops of ammonia. Do not use detergent-enhanced ammonia!

Throughout the winter, check the container once or twice a week, verifying the temperature and that the water has not evaporated to expose the media. Use an ammonia test kit to be sure to maintain a reading of 1 to 3 ppm. When the test reading drops below that level, add several more drops of ammonia to "feed" the bacteria. After the first several weeks of operation, your bacteria will have revived in the warmer temperature and be oxidizing the ammonia food.

In the spring, once the water temperature has warmed above 50°F, you can set up your bio-filter with the media and colony you have kept established through the winter. Your bio-filter is immediately up and running a full three to four weeks before it would be if started from scratch.

CHAPTER FIVE

Fish Health

Taking good care of your fish is the best medicine you can give them. Photo of Joe Zuritsky's Koi in Philadelphia, Pennsylvania

The best way to tend to the good health of your fish is to practice preventive maintenance. Pond fish can be deceptively forgiving. You may not notice that conditions have deteriorated until one or more fish turns belly-up. Regular water testing may be the best friend your fish could have. Often the first clue that something is amiss is the subtle sign of stress—blushing or a pink cast appearing in the fins and tail. For that reason alone, I strongly recommend including a white fish among your pet collection. Nearly everything that can go wrong in a pond, from water quality to fish illness or parasitic attack, is accompanied by fish stress. Besides telltale blushing that turns into red-veining and hemorrhaging in the skin, fish also slough off their slime coating during times of stress. This can be disastrous, as the slime coat harbors important enzymes that fight disease and parasites. A clue that this is happening is the appearance of a thin, whitish coating on the surface of the pond water. If you notice either of these signs of hidden stress, test your water first. Once you have ruled out complications arising from water quality–pH, ammonia, nitrite, nitrate, low levels of dissolved oxygen, or the presence of hydrogen sulfide–you can begin addressing other possible sources of the problem, including the critical issue of fish load in the pond. Dr. Erik Johnson estimates that 90 percent of fish health problems are directly related to too much fish load in the pond.

Koi veterinarian Dr. Erik Johnson estimates that 90 percent of fish health problems are directly related to too great a fish load in the pond.

Fish Behavior–Clues to Problems

Flashing

When a fish "flashes," it is rubbing an irritated part of its body on the pond bottom, the pond sides, or on the side of a plant pot. Flashing usually indicates the presence of parasites such as flukes; however, it can also indicate pH changes or a reaction to a water change. Chlorine presence, for example, will cause irritation and the flashing behavior. When your fish flashes, check it closely for parasites, remembering to consider water quality as well. If the flashing occurs only at a certain time of day, the problem is probably pH. If the fish are flashing throughout the day, parasites are likely the reason.

Laying Over

The fish appears lethargic, listing to its side at the pond bottom. This is not normal. First, check the water for pH and ammonia. Next, check the fish for parasites or a wound. You will probably need to clean the pond and treat the water with a three percent salt solution.

Clamped Fins

While fish adjust their fins in swimming, a fish keeping its fins tightly clamped to its body communicates displeasure with its environmental conditions. Test the water to determine what is affecting the fish—ammonia, nitrite, nitrate, pH. Check the fish for parasites.

Isolating Behavior

Koi and goldfish are sociable, schooling fish. The fish that isolates itself from the crowd, hovering or sulking unhappily in a corner or at the bottom of the pond, has a problem. Since other pondmates are swimming happily, net the unhappy fish and keep it in a quarantine tank where you can observe it closely to determine the problem. Often the fish that isolates itself may be picked on by its tankmates. This behavior is not the same as the bumping and chasing of males after a female during spawning.

Gasping at Surface

This can be due to any of several causes–low dissolved oxygen in the water, low pH, or the presence of ammonia or nitrite. First, test your water for pH, ammonia, and nitrite. If none is the problem, aerate the water. Also, check the water temperature. If it is warmer than 86°F, do a partial water exchange to cool it enough to hold more oxygen. If you can test your dissolved oxygen levels in the pond, you will have a better idea of the problem. While fish can survive concentrations testing between 5 and 7, these concentrations can weaken them over an extended period of time, making them susceptible to other health problems. You may need to clean the pond bottom of accumulated organic wastes to enhance oxygen levels further, since decomposition by aerobic bacteria removes oxygen from the water. If pH seems to be the problem, consider its cause. You may need to supply buffers to the water, as well as additional aeration. Whatever the cause, the pond probably has too many fish.

Not Eating

During peak pond season, healthy fish are hungry. A fish that shows no interest in food, choosing instead to remain off somewhere by itself, has a problem. Fish troubled with parasites continue to feed. Bacterial infections produce a lack of interest in food. Remove the fish to a quarantine tank and observe it closely. If the fish has an open wound, you can treat it with antibiotic ointment. The fish that refuses to eat at all needs professional attention, microscopic analysis, and antibiotics. Fish with bacterial infections that will eat can be given medicated food.

Large Fish Die and Small Survive

This usually indicates low dissolved oxygen levels in the pond. Add more aeration. Consider fish load, water temperature, and water pH.

Small Fish Die and Large Survive

This usually indicates nitrite poisoning. Check your fish for the stress signs–fin and tail blushing. Test the water for nitrites. You may have to perform a partial water exchange of up to 40 percent and treat the pond with a three percent salt solution to alleviate nitrite poisoning.

Darting and Bashing into Walls

This usually indicates the water pH is too low. You may need to buffer the pond water. (See Chapter 4.)

Jumping

Goldfish and koi do not typically jump from the water. Jumping indicates the presence of parasites, discomfort with the water, or electric shocks. In the case of shocks, the jumping is accompanied by frantic and/or erratic swimming. Because shocks are the most immediate of possible causes, turn off all electricity going to the pond to see if the behavior stops. Do not touch the water until the electricity has been shut off! If the fish calm down, check your electrical system and be sure it is attached to a ground fault circuit system. If your pond does not have such a system, portable GFCS units are available that can be plugged into your outdoor outlet. The pond attachments are then plugged into the GFCS.

If electricity is not the problem, test the water for ammonia, nitrite, and pH. After ruling out water quality, inspect the fish for parasites and administer salt or an appropriate treatment.

Water Quality Factors Affecting Fish Health

Water Temperature

Water temperature is critical to fish health for three primary reasons. The slime coating, which contains the fish immune system, does not function below 60°F, while bacteria and parasites are viable to 50°F or even

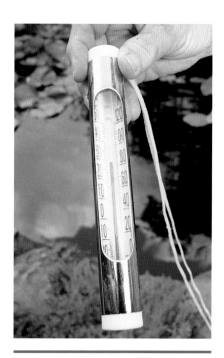

A submersible pond thermometer allows you to check the water temperature in the pond. A reading of 84°F is quite high–close to the maximum safe temperature for feeding fish. It may be necessary to execute a partial water exchange to cool the water.

The Living Pond

cooler. Avoid handling or stressing fish at temperatures below 60°F.

Second, water at temperatures above 86°F holds significantly less oxygen than at lower temperatures. This can drastically affect fish health, particularly if organic wastes are processed by bacteria within the pond or if you feed your fish, generating greater oxygen needs.

Third, sudden changes in water temperature greater than one or two degrees per hour seriously stress fish and put them at risk. During early spring and autumn, when the weather may change drastically

Attach your pond thermometer to a string so you can test the water temperature at one-third the depth of the pond.

from one day to the next, you may wish to use a thermostatically controlled heater in the pond to regulate the temperature and maintain the water at 65°F until the weather stabilizes in safe ranges for the fish.

Chlorine

Chlorine kills fish. Even low levels cause irreversible gill damage. Treat all water additions in excess of five percent of the pond's volume with a dechlor product or with a solution you have prepared yourself: 130 grams of sodium thiosulfate in one liter of water makes a stock solution that you can safely store for use as needed. Use two drops of the stock solution per gallon of water to be treated.

Chloramine

The danger of chloramine combines the deadly threat of chlorine with the added presence of potentially fish-toxic levels of ammonia. If the water is added to water with an active bio-filter, monitor the ammonia level to be sure the filter is accommodating the addition. You may note a slight spike in ammonia that quickly vanishes. Test the water pH. Ammonia ionizes below pH readings of 7.4, converting to a less toxic

presence. If the water contains salt, you cannot remedy the ammonia presence with zeolite since the zeolite then releases rather than absorbs ammonia. Use a reputable commercial product that reduces toxic ammonia to its less toxic ammonium form. Unless you have a test kit for ammonium, the usual water test kit for ammonia levels will reflect both the toxic and non-toxic forms.

Ammonia

Ammonia is produced as a waste product by fish. It also is a by-product of aerobic decomposition of organic wastes. Ammonia presence is due primarily to too many fish in the system or to an inadequately functioning or inaccurately sized bio-filter. Ammonia causes the skin of a fish to redden and damages or "burns" fish gills. Ammonia-affected fish display clamped fins, blushing of the fins and tail, and isolation behavior. They also lie on the pond bottom, hang just below the water surface, wiggle their tails, and produce excess slime. Even low levels of ammonia, considered merely "safe," can depress the immune system of a fish. *Any* presence of ammonia in the water should not tolerated.

If ammonia is present in your pond water, check the pH. If necessary, do up to a 40 percent water exchange, adding salt at a rate of one tablespoon per gallon of pond volume. (Be sure to account for any salt already present in the pond.) Zeolite can be used to absorb ammonia from the water as long as no salt is present in the water. Commercial products that change toxic ammonia to the less toxic ammonium can also be used. If the water pH is complicating the problem, explore possible causes and consider buffering the pond water.

Nitrite

Nitrite is produced within the nitrogen cycle by *Nitrosomonas* bacteria-reducing ammonia.

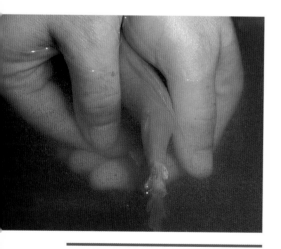

Water quality may be the cause of many fish health problems. This fish displays a kinked back and a rotted tail. With the water so dirty, chances are bacteria and parasites are thriving and can easily attack the weakened fish. Photo by Ron Everhart

Like ammonia, its detected presence is usually the result of too many fish or because the filter system is too small or is not functioning properly. It is highly toxic to fish. Known as brown blood disease, it prevents red blood cells from carrying oxygen and causes the fish to suffocate and die. Initial signs of nitrite presence are the usual stress signs, blushing fins and tail. The gills also flare widely and the fish seems to hyperventilate. By the time the body displays red-veining and hemorrhages under the skin, it is probably too late to save the fish.

Regularly testing the pond water will alert you to a growing nitrite presence. At the first sign of nitrite, execute partial water changes, up to 40 percent. Add one teaspoon of non-iodized salt per gallon of pond volume to inhibit the fish's uptake of the toxic nitrite.

Nitrate

Nitrate does not usually create problems for your fish, especially if your pond or filter system provides aquatic plants to use it. Ponds treated with the algicide Simazine may experience raised levels of nitrate accumulation. Fish affected by excessive nitrate presence appear lethargic and remain on the pond bottom. They may

also display lesions around their mouths and keep their fins tightly clamped to their bodies. Remove Simazine, if present, as you execute partial water changes to 40 percent. Avoid future buildups with aquatic plants such as water hyacinth kept within floating net protectors or in the top of your filter system.

Dissolved Oxygen

Dissolved oxygen does not exist in the pond by itself. It is part of the water molecule. The number of oxygen-holding molecules within the pond water is closely related to the pH, to the amount of plants growing in the water, and to the water temperature. Your pond water should test with at least 5 ppm of oxygen to allow short-term survival of your fish. The desired level of oxygen presence is over 8 ppm.

If the water pH measures below neutral, there are more free hydrogen ions in the water, each of them not part of a molecule holding oxygen. (The free oxygen escapes into the air.) The result: lower oxygen availability for your fish. Your fish will gasp at the surface or remain at the waterfall during the day.

If the pond is heavily planted with aquatic plants, the plants produce oxygen during daytime photosynthesis and use oxygen during nighttime respiration. Too many plants results in lowered oxygen levels early in the morning. Again, fish will gasp at the surface or remain at the waterfall early in the morning.

If the water's temperature is over 86°F, the water can hold less oxygen. Again, oxygen atoms escape into the air and hydrogen ions remain free. In extended periods of warm water, the water's pH may be affected. Once again, fish will gasp at the surface or stay at the waterfall during the day.

To increase oxygen: aerate with an air pump and stone, hook up a venturi attachment to the pond, or as a temporary, emergency solution, treat with hydrogen peroxide at a rate of one half to one cup per hundred gallons. You can also spray the hydrogen peroxide into the pond at a rate of 60 squirts per 100 gallons, taking care not to spray directly at or even close to your fish. Hydrogen peroxide is effective for only three to four hours.

Hydrogen Sulfide (H₂S)

Hydrogen sulfide is toxic to fish. It is the by-product of anaerobic bacteria working to decompose organic matter within the layer of sediment that builds up on the pond bottom or that builds up unseen within sand, gravel, or stone on the bottom of the system. It can also occur in filter systems in which sediment has been allowed to accumulate. These anaerobic bacteria use sulfur in their metabolic process to produce the hydrogen sulfide. While a test kit for its presence exists, you can suspect its presence if you have a layer of gravel or rocks in your pond bottom or if you can actually see the mulm buildup on the pond bottom. Disturbing the substrate produces the smell of rotten eggs, or the pond water may exude the foul odor.

Under such conditions, the only solution is to remove all fish immediately to safe waters and to fully drain and clean the pond. Even this may not save the fish. Do not attempt to clean the gravel with the fish still in the pond; you will only release more hydrogen sulfide in the process, which will probably kill any remaining fish. (Potassium permanganate can be used to degrade hydrogen sulfide if applied at 1–2 ppm to reduce it to nontoxic compounds and further oxidize the detritus that is feeding the anaerobic bacteria. Such a remedy requires a full knowledge of the caustic compound. Research it very carefully!) Resorting to "sludge-eating" bacteria once the hydrogen sulfide is being produced in the pond is an insufficient remedy applied too late.

Toxic Runoffs

Improperly siting a pond allows surface runoff of water containing pesticides or herbicides from nearby grounds. As a precaution, do not use chemicals around your pond. Likewise, be careful of spray applications that might be windborne. Another toxin that might enter your pond water and risk your fish is arsenic from pressure-treated wood. Do not use pressure-treated wood where water might flow over it and enter the pond. Fish behavior that might indicate the presence of a toxic element in the water include the usual stress signs as well as erratic swimming, jumping, and, in progressed cases, growth deformities. If toxic elements enter your pond's water, remove fish to temporary quarters and fully drain and clean the pond.

Copper and Simazine

Copper sulfate is still a common remedy for algae in farm ponds. It is never appropriate for use in your garden/fish pond. Obviously, it will kill plants. Even more sinister is its effect on fish. Copper sulfate strips fish of their protective slime coating, leaving them vulnerable to parasites and disease.

Be careful not to use copper pipes or ornaments in your pond. The copper leaches into the water, possibly creating a bluish cast to the water. The effect on plants and fish is the same as that of copper sulfate.

Simazine is a similar algae control. Supposedly safe for fish, accumulations create nitrate problems indicated by fin injection, red mouth lesions, and lethargy. Obviously, it is not safe for aquatic plants— both algae and others! If Simazine is used to control algae, take care to remove it through regular water changes.

A quarantine tank setup for koi: large quarters, filtration and aeration, and protective netting over the top.

Treating Fish Health Problems

Quarantine Tank

Any new fish to be introduced into your pond should be held in a quarantine tank for two to three weeks before being added to your pond population. This assures you of the health of your new pet and protects the health of its future pondmates. A quarantine tank is also used for tending sick fish. Many fish keepers keep their quarantine tank set up between uses, maintaining the active biological system with one or two small fish. Bob Bon Giorno recommends adding a small "kamikaze koi" to the quarantine tank to speed recovery of a sick koi since they are naturally a schooling fish. The same holds true for goldfish.

THE TANK
A quarantine tank may be as small as a 10-gallon aquarium for small koi and goldfish, or it may be as large as a five-foot or greater, portable pond commonly used in koi shows. Provide netting over the top of the tank to prevent the fish from jumping out. The fish will feel less stressed if you also provide a hiding place within the tank.

Even a piece of floating Styrofoam grants the fish peace of mind.

THE FILTER
Set up your quarantine tank with a bio-filter to control ammonia created by the presence of fish. Do not use zeolite as a media in the filter if you will be treating the water with salt. (Salt will cause the zeolite to release its ammonia store.) Likewise, do not use carbon as a medium in the filter, as it quickly removes any medications from the water. Simple foam or sponges are all that is needed.

THE WATER
Perform daily ammonia tests on the water to be sure the filter is functioning. The pH should be at or above neutral (7.4). You may wish to use crushed oyster shell in the bottom of the tank to buffer the water if the pH reads on the low side of 7.4.

Add one tablespoon of non-iodized salt per gallon of water (2.5 pounds per 100 gallons) to create the desired three percent salt solution. This will promote fish production of the slime coat that contains essential enzymes to fight off disease and parasites. This level of salt will also take care of many parasite problems. Crustacean parasites such as *Lernea* (anchor worm) and *Argulus* (lice) can be controlled by adding a few drops of

Methylene Blue to a very pale blue tint or by adding one quarter of a teaspoon of Dimilin per 100 gallons. Use Fluke Tabs if you detect flukes.

Provide supplemental aeration with an air pump and a long bar stone. This is especially important if you medicate the water.

WATER TEMPERATURE
To introduce new fish from their transport to their new home, float the bag containing the fish or mix pond water into the transport container water until the temperatures have equalized. Fish are stressed by rapid temperature changes.

If you treat a fish removed from the cold pond waters of autumn, winter, or spring, raise the water temperature only one degree per hour until it is 72°F, at which point you can begin the hospital treatment. Handle the fish as little as possible in cold temperatures since handling removes the protective slime coating. The immune system within the coating does not resume until water temperatures are above 60°F. Many pathogens that attack your fish are active down to 50°F.

Dips and Baths

Dips involve immersing fish in a treatment tank/aquarium that is dosed appropriately, the fish

remaining in the solution for a maximum of 7 to 10 minutes. A dip may be as quick as holding the net containing the fish within the solution to a count of ten. Often dips are performed as a series of immersions 12 hours apart. Medications and remedies usually suggest how long the dip should last. If the fish appears distressed by the experience, shorten the dip and return the fish to the quarantine tank. A dipped fish may appear weak but should not be flipped over.

The safest dip treatment for fish is a salt dip of 10 tablespoons of non-iodized salt dissolved in a gallon of water, or 50 tablespoons to 5 gallons of water. The dipping may last up to 10 minutes, provided the fish is not stressed. Repeating

Aeration in the quarantine tank is critical, and not just for the basic oxygen needs of the fish. Many medicines used to treat fish require vigorous aeration since they use available oxygen to work (oxidization).

A thermometer helps you monitor critical water temperatures for proper treatment in your quarantine tank.

Oil of clove, at a rate of 5 to 10 drops per gallon of water, is used to anesthetize fish.

The anesthesia has taken effect when the fish lolls on its side, breathing slowly, but still displaying eye reflexes.

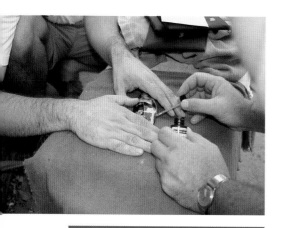

Working quickly with the anesthetized fish out of water, one person holds the fish securely and the other performs treatment.

the dip two more times at 12-hour intervals remedies most parasites.

A bath, on the other hand, uses a weaker strength of medicine, but the fish stay immersed in the solution for 6 to 8 hours.

Anesthetizing

Removing anchor worms or treating wounds on smaller goldfish can usually be performed by holding the fish gently but firmly within the hand. Treating a larger fish, however, requires that the fish be placed on a flat and secure surface for treatment. Two people are usually required to work efficiently, with one person holding the fish and the other person performing the treatment, and then the fish is returned promptly to the water. Even with two people, the fish may need to be sedated or calmed enough to perform the treatment.

Oil of clove, at a dosage of 5 to 10 drops per gallon in a tub, will tranquilize a large fish in 10 to 15 minutes. Although the fish displays muscle tone and eye reflexes, it respires slowly. Remove the fish from the water and work quickly. Holding the fish firmly to prevent it from falling accidentally, you may also wish to cover its eyes with your hand. When you have finished, return the fish to fresh water and guide it by hand so it

remains upright until recovered enough from the anesthesia to swim by itself. Recovery from the tranquilizer usually takes 10 to 15 minutes.

Salt

Non-iodized or sea salt is an ideal remedy for many fish health problems because it can treat a problem without harming the environment, doesn't cause stress to the fish, doesn't harm the bio-filter, and is inexpensive. Use salt, however, only *after* testing your water and correcting any water-quality problems. If, for example, the problem is nitrite poisoning and you must perform a 40 percent water change, wait until the 40 percent has been removed before treating the new water with salt. Salt can be used in the quarantine tank and in the pond itself. Salt does not evaporate or dissipate; it is removed with water changes. Repeated use of salt in the pond can result in an accumulation and a concentration higher than you desire. A salinity test kit is advised.

Always monitor your fish during treatment and immediately following to be certain you have remedied the problem. For example, if you use salt to treat fish displaying flashing behavior and the flashing continues after two days of salt use, the problem is probably flukes, which are resistant to salt treatment and require a different treatment.

In most cases you would use a three percent solution of salt. Dissolve the non-iodized salt in a five-gallon bucket and distribute it evenly around the pond. It is best to administer this dosage over a three-day period, or at least over three 12-hour increments, to avoid shocking your filter or the fish. For a 3 percent solution, use:

1. One teaspoon per gallon daily for three days, for a total of three teaspoons, or one tablespoon, per gallon.

2. One pound per hundred gallons added daily for three days, for a total dose of three pounds per hundred gallons.

At the recommended 3 percent solution, salt:

1. Rids fish of most parasites, except flukes and the encysted stage of ich.

2. Inhibits uptake of harmful nitrites by fish.

3. Somewhat inhibits uptake of ammonia by the fish and so minimizes gill and tissue damage.

4. Stimulates slime coat production by fish.

5. Reduces the influx of water into the fish (osmoregulation); too much water intake can damage kidneys, and stress may invite bacteria infestations.

6. Kills algae.

"Kills algae" contains a clue to pondkeepers who have plants in the pond. Salt in the water, known as brackish water, is not suited to many freshwater aquatic plants. Submerged plants will not tolerate it at all, and many water lilies are sensitive to salt. Cattails, water irises, and water hyacinths will tolerate brief stints in brackish water. If you will use salt in the pond, remove plants prior to treatment or when you notice their protests of yellowing foliage.

Because salt is so effective at eliminating parasite problems that attack your fish in the cooler waters of autumn and spring, before the fish's immune system is up and running, you may decide to provide salt to the autumn water change and again with the spring water change. Obviously, plants would have to be kept elsewhere until the pond is desalinated. Even hardy water lilies can be stored over the winter outside the pond. Hardy marginal aquatics can be set into garden holes dug up to their pot tops.

Always dissolve salt first before adding it in solution. Fish can burn their bellies if they rest too close to a dissolving pile of salt on the pond bottom.

Potassium Permanganate

Because salt is harmful to plants, you may wish to use potassium permanganate instead. Potassium permanganate is an oxidizing chemical that is highly toxic to fish in even small overdoses. It is also carcinogenic in humans. You must wear special clothing, eye protection, and gloves when working with it. Being a controlled substance, it is available only through limited sources. Its use is quite specific as to dosage and application. It is, however, highly effective in medical treatments of fish, in disinfecting plants of snails and parasites, and in remedying the problems associated with hydrogen sulfide. If you plan to use this dangerous substance, consult a responsible expert for accurate information on proper use and safety precautions.

Water Changes

Changing the water, preferably by partial water exchange of up to 40 percent of the pond volume, is often recommended to remedy fish health problems, particularly those associated with water quality. Water changes are also necessary to remove salt from the pond water since it does not evaporate and accumulates with each additional treatment. Regular water exchanges of five to 25

Potassium permanganate is an oxidant that must be aerated vigorously. It is a highly toxic chemical, so scrupulous care and an exact dosage are crucial.

percent are often a part of regular pond maintenance, too, especially in conjunction with pond vacuums. Perform water exchanges with care to protect the health of your fish.

Consider how the added water affects the temperature of the pond. Changing the temperature around your fish by one degree per hour is considered safe. If the water you would add is significantly different in temperature, add the water in portions throughout the day in order not to shock the fish. (This procedure may be necessary for summer ponds with water temperatures over 86°F that need to cool down.) Monitor the water temperature during such exchanges with a submersible thermometer.

Consider how the added water affects the total alkalinity of your pond's water. Alkalinity refers to the bicarbonate concentration or buffering capacity of the water. Water testing in the lower than neutral pH range usually has a deficiency of bicarbonates and requires buffering. Such water produces stress in fish and, eventually, death. Baking soda (sodium bicarbonate), crushed oyster shell, or crushed limestone provides buffering. Consider, at the same time, the pH levels of the existing pond water and of the water you are adding. Ideally, you want your pond pH between 7.2 to 8.0, with 7.4 considered optimum for koi.

If you are executing a major water change of 30 or 40 percent of the pond volume, you may wish to add a teaspoon of salt per gallon of water to alleviate stress in the fish. Remember that most aquatic plants do not appreciate such salinity and will not thrive or survive.

Common Diseases of Goldfish and Koi

Common Fish Diseases

Anchor worm—*Lernaea carasii* is actually a very small aquatic crustacean that at the parasitic stage of its life attaches its anchor-shaped head to the body of the fish, usually near the fins or tail. The worm looks like a tiny white stick protruding from the fish. (It is usually an egg-laden female feeding off the fish.) The worm soon produces an irritation and a bloody red spot. Remove it very carefully with tweezers, grasping the worm firmly behind its head where it is attached to the fish. Gently pull it free of the fish and swab the wound with seven percent tincture of iodine. Be very careful removing anchor worms from the eye area of the fish. Treat the pond three times in early spring with Dipterex or Dimilin 25W at seven-day intervals, to take into account the life cycle of the parasite. Anchor worms are treatable in water only during the free-swimming stage. If you are treating a full pond, remove any remaining medication from the water through charcoal filtration. You can more easily treat the entire pond with a three percent salt solution that is left in the pond for three weeks to accommodate the parasite's life cycle. Birds are the vector of pond anchor worms, and snails may act as the intermediary hosts. Preventive control involves keeping both birds and snails out of the pond. Anchor worm affects koi and goldfish.

Chilodinella–A microscopic parasite, this is one of the fastest fish killers in the cold water of the early spring pond. Symptoms include a large number of fish dying on the surface of the water and fish lying on their sides, making mad dashes when disturbed. Provide supplemental aeration and a three percent salt solution in the pond for 14 days. Gill damage is common among survivors. Chilodinella is primarily a koi problem.

Costia–*Ichthyobodo necatrix* is a ciliated protozoan parasite that can kill koi quickly in the colder waters of spring and autumn when the fish immune system is shut down. Like other parasites, costia may be free-swimming or attached to the fish. Fins redden and breathing is labored in affected fish. Spiderweb lesions and excess mucus also indicate the infestation. Treat with three percent salt solution. Preventive treatment is to prepare the autumn

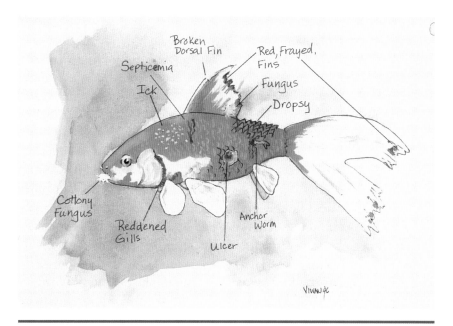

The Primary Disease and Parasite Problems of Goldfish
Drawing by Vivian McCord

pond with a three percent salt solution and repeating it with the spring opening of the koi pond.

Dropsy–Also called pine-cone disease because the fish scales protrude from the body, due to the pressure of accumulated fluid. Dropsy is bacterial but does not seem to be infectious, although it is often fatal. Some experts speculate that it results from bacteria attracted to food rotting in the fish's intestinal tract during the slowed metabolism of cold waters. Treat with antibiotics. Dropsy affects koi and goldfish.

Epistylis–Cottony tufts appear on fish skin, especially around the mouth, fins, and tail. This

disease is often confused with *Saprolegnia* fungal attacks that occur in the terminal stages of other health problems. Epistylis is quite treatable with a three percent salt solution, and the fish respond within a couple days. Epistylis affects koi and goldfish.

Fish lice–*Argulus* fasten themselves flat against the body of the fish and may not be noticeable unless you check after noticing your fish rubbing against pot sides or the pond walls (flashing). Treating the entire pond with a three percent salt solution will kill them. You can also use Dipterex or Dimilin 25W. Fish lice affect koi and goldfish.

Turtle Ponds

Turtles make for interesting pond pets.

The Incredible Turtle

Turtles are fascinating creatures. They are reptiles of unique appearance. All species possess a shell, either soft or hard. "Hinges" in some terrestrial species allow the turtle to

Even aquatic turtles need a place to bask in the sun. This Pseudemys floridana hoyi, *a member of the* Emydidae *family, is commonly found in Florida.*

retreat within its shell and tightly close the "doors." The upper shell is called the carapace; the lower half, or underside, is called the plastron. Some species, such as the box turtle, are terrestrial and need only a source of water in their habitat. Others, like the red-ear or the painted turtle, are semi-aquatic and need at least a small swimming pond with sun-bathing and winter hibernation facilities. The soft-shell turtle and the snapping turtle are the only truly aquatic turtles you might keep. Before you consider setting up a turtle pond, check with your state's department of natural resources. The box turtle *(Terrapene carolina)*, for example, is protected in several states and not allowed for even private keeping. All sea turtles, besides being saltwater turtles, are protected.

Most turtles are omnivores and prefer meat. Mature adults may eat more vegetables, but they still maintain interest in the living protein found in the water–primarily your fish.

Keeping turtles within your water garden/fish pond means not only are you unlikely to see many baby fish in your pond, you may have to contend with actual bites taken out of larger fish. Turtles do best in their own pond with guppies, minnows, or feeder goldfish supplying their protein needs.

Keeping turtles in their own pond also makes maintenance easier. Because turtles both feed and defecate within the water, the water quickly becomes polluted. Water color and odor indicate whether the water is becoming fouled by bacteria in feces and decomposing organic matter. The primary health threat is from *Salmonella*, a bacteria that causes illness similar to typhoid fever. *Salmonella* bacteria are always present, but their danger rests only in the concentration that naturally occurs with accumulations of fecal matter and decomposing food. Frequent water changes are necessary in keeping turtles to prevent this infection. In an indoor aquarium, such water changes may be needed every week or two. Outside turtle ponds, being larger, may need water changes only once a month. Borrowing from the koi-keeping hobby, a bottom drain may enhance the desirable, clean habitat conditions.

Turtles do not have teeth. Instead they have powerful beaks strong enough to tear apart fibrous plant material. If you feed your turtle strictly on soft foods for any length of time, its beak may become overgrown and require trimming.

All turtles *must* have calcium for bone and shell growth. Carnivorous turtles benefit from animal bone in their diet, such as fish bones. Turtles also need Vitamin D to facilitate the absorption of the calcium. Either provide nutritional enhancement of their food or be sure that they have access to direct sunlight. (Remember that glass stops most UV rays and prevents them from accessing this necessary nutrient.) Never carry a turtle by its tail; you can damage or kill it.

Hibernation and Estivation

Reptiles that live in places where freezing occurs cope by hibernating. With their food supply reduced and the ground frozen, their winter survival is further hampered because they have no internal control of body heat. Like other reptiles, their metabolic rate lowers and they seek refuge until living conditions improve. Some turtles hibernate under water in mud, and some crawl into holes dug by other animals or by themselves. Still others burrow into the earth or into mulch piles.

Sensing the days' shortening and the nights' cooler temperatures, they begin looking for safe napping quarters. You can help by turning over the soil to a necessary depth, by digging holes, or by providing piles of mulch—whatever is the preferred respite of the breed you keep. Your outdoor turtle needs hibernation quarters deeper than your frost line. With its heartbeat and respiration slowing, the turtle will

Include a place in your turtle habitat where this unique pet can dig in to spend quiet times of hibernation and estivation undisturbed.

tuck itself in. It will survive through its hibernation on stored body fat until the weather warms again in the spring.

Turtles kept indoors should be kept awake 365 days a year. As the days grow shorter, provide extra warmth and longer daylight hours with artificial light. Turtles needs to be fully awake to feed. In a halfway state between wakefulness and hibernation, turtles are not able to assimilate food. In semi-wakefulness, a turtle's body consumes more energy, which depletes it of stored body fat and risks starvation.

Estivation is a function used by turtles to cope with hot and dry conditions. When a turtle estivates, it digs deep into the earth, where its metabolism slows in a quiet rest until moisture again becomes available. Gopher tortoises in desert habitats may estivate several times in a year for a month or two if water or food is in short supply.

Metabolism

Turtles live life at a slow, slow pace. This involves much more than simple movement. Having no internal temperature control and with only a three-chambered heart, compared to the four-chambered versions of warm-blooded animals, they are considered cold-blooded. This allows them to go without food for extended periods when they are inactive, such as during hibernation and estivation. They can also go without breathing for extended periods. Even a terrestrial box turtle can remain underwater for an hour without drowning. Likewise, aquatic turtles hibernating underwater can manage until spring without coming up for air.

Respiration

All turtles have lungs, but they cannot push air in and out as do animals with diaphragms and rib cages. With their "ribs" fused together to form a shell, air is moved in and out of their lungs by movements of their limbs and throat. Also, moving the head in and out of the shell produces a pumping action that aids in breathing.

Even aquatic turtles do not have gills, but they do have tiny blood vessels within the thin skin lining the insides of their throats, the pharyngeal cavity. Functioning much like the gills of a fish, it pulls oxygen from the water to enable the aquatic species to remain underwater for long periods. Combined with a slowed metabolism, turtles can even hibernate buried in mud under water. This special capability is called pharyngeal respiration.

Types of Turtle

Although there are over 200 species of turtles throughout the world, you will not keep any of the six species of sea turtles, any species of giant tortoises, or any of the endangered and protected species. Likewise, turtles requiring very specific habitat (turtles regarded as delicate or difficult to keep) would not be considered by the novice turtle keeper.

Generally, terrestrial or land turtles need less care since their feces tend to dry up and the odors and risks of decay and disease associated with warm water are not present. Semiaquatics are more active, often spending as much time out of the water as in it. Aquatic turtles are for the most part mean and ugly. The type of turtle you keep determines the habitat you create.

Aquatic Turtles

SNAPPING TURTLE
The only fully aquatic turtle that you might keep is one of the two species of snapping turtle, the alligator snapper (*Macroclemys temmincki*) or the common snapper (*Chelydra serpentina*). Both are mean and ugly. With very strong jaws, they are very dangerous pets to

The snapping turtle, while a true aquatic species, has such a nasty disposition and poses such real physical threat that he is not likely to be considered a potential pet for your turtle pond. Photo by Ron Everhart

keep! They are not recommended for keeping as pets. The most distinguishing characteristic of the common snapping turtle is its prominent beak and zigzag edge at the back of its shell. Looking down on it, you won't notice its eyes. The alligator snapper, its name deceptive since it is found as far north as central Illinois, is one of the world's largest turtles, sometimes weighing over two hundred pounds. Weights in the 30- to 50-pound range are common. Snappers are voracious eaters and can wipe out whole ponds of baby ducklings or snatch a finger. They get along with no other species, including their own. They may overcome initial shyness, but they never become tame.

MUD, MUSK, AND SOFT-SHELLED TURTLES

Musk turtles (*Sternotherus*, also known as "stinkpots") and mud turtles (*Kinosternon*), known as soft-shelled turtles, make good pets once they are tamed. Until they are accustomed to you, however, they will emit a most unpleasant smell, much like that of a skunk. Both species are climbers, often basking in trees in the wild. The most commonly encountered soft-shells in the U.S. are the *Trionyx spinifer*, the spiny soft-shell, and the smooth soft-shell, *Trionyx muticus*, which is slightly smaller.

Although spending most of their time in the water, these turtles do need a dry basking perch. They eat underwater, preferring meat and fish, but they also eat crustaceans, insects, snails, mussels, worms, and some succulent vegetation.

Handle soft-shells very carefully—they scratch and bite without provocation. Keep no more than two, preferably just one, as their sharp claws can injure the soft shells of companions. Their soft shells make them a poor companion with other species, too.

Their pond bottom should be bare or covered with coarse gravel. Supply their favorite, a piece of driftwood, for a basking perch. Change the water frequently, especially if you feed heavily, which they prefer. Attaining sizes greater than a foot across, sometimes

The soft-shelled turtle is the one fully aquatic turtle you might keep. This smooth-shelled Trionyx muticus *is one of two species commonly found in the U.S. Photo by Ron Everhart*

18 inches in female specimens, they require considerable space. A filtration system to accommodate their wastes would encompass 10 cubic feet. Mud turtles, growing to around six inches across, require considerably less space.

Feed them earthworms, lean beef, fish fillets, shrimp, live fish, crayfish, crabs, crickets, grasshoppers, snails, mussels, dog food, and liver.

Semiaquatic Turtles

SPOTTED TURTLE

Clemmys guttata, the spotted turtle, is a pleasant pet of the Emydid family, growing to five inches with a smooth, black carapace marked with small yellow spots. The underside or plastron is yellow with black blotches. A hardy species, it eats insects, earthworms, carrion, and very few vegetables. You can feed captive specimens dog food, too. They are one of the most available species in North America.

RED-EAR TURTLE

Because *Pseudemys scripta*, the red-ear turtle of the large Emydidae family, was once commonly sold (the "dime-store" turtle), it may be found anywhere in the U.S. Members of this group of turtles are known as red-eared turtles, yellow-

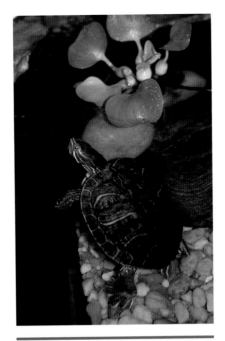

The red-ear turtle, or red-eared slider, is one of the most popular of turtle pets.

bellied turtles, Cumberland turtles, Rio Grande turtles, red-bellied turtles, cooters, and sliders. Some of the species are commonly found in and around brackish water. Hence, they take well to salt dips to control parasites.

Their shells are mutely patterned, the scales shedding in growth. With webbed feet and no hinges on the plastron, they are conspicuously marked with yellow and green. The males have long claws. Subspecies of this group may have red or yellow plastrons. These turtles may grow to 12 to 15 inches.

Omnivorous as juveniles, these turtles tend to eat more vegetable matter as they

mature. Kept in a water garden, they nibble on your fish in their youth and then turn to your plants as they mature. All eat underwater. Feed them raw fish, earthworms, chicken liver, melon, and lettuce. Commonly kept pets, they are docile and easy to tame.

PAINTED TURTLE

Chrysemys picta, the painted turtle, wears a smooth, blackish hard shell with no hinges or sawtooth edges. The edges of the shell are marked with red bands and bars that extend into the underside of the carapace. The top of the shell, which may grow to seven inches, is blackish with distinctive markings of red bands and bars on the margin of the top and on the underside of the carapace. The plastron is yellow, sometimes marked with irregular black blotches. Their tails are slender,

Painted turtles are sometimes confused with the red-eared family, being commonly available and making pleasant pets. Photo by Ron Everhart

the feet webbed, and the males possess long claws.

Like other semiaquatic turtles, they prefer to eat underwater. Feed them low-fat protein foods of earthworms, tadpoles, whole small fish, crickets, grasshoppers, crayfish, mussels, clams, snails, and chicken liver.

DIAMONDBACK TERRAPIN

Diamondback terrapins, *Malaclemys terrapin*, are never found far from salt water. In setting up a habitat for these beautiful turtles, maintain their water at a 3.5 sea water salinity, multiplying $1/3 \times 3.5\% \times 128$ ounces of salt for every gallon of water. Sea salt provides important trace elements. With brackish water, they are unlikely to be troubled by parasites.

Pale gray in color, they wear darker gray or black spots or blotches on their heads, necks, and legs. The sculptured carapace is saw-toothed and bears knobs across its center. The plastron is not hinged. Webbed feet note them as swimmers, but they do need a basking site in which to dry out and sun themselves.

Feed them in the water. They appreciate mussels, small oysters, and soft-shelled clams. You can also feed them snails, shrimp, small crabs, and crayfish. Shy pets, they are nonetheless enjoyable.

WOOD TURTLE

Wood turtles, *Clemmys insculpta*, wear shells even more deeply sculptured than the those of the diamondback terrapin. They are native to damp woodlands in the Northeast and westward to Wisconsin. Technically considered terrestrial turtles, they spend as much time in the water as they do out, eating and breeding in water. Encountered on a woodland trail, they may pull in their heads and limbs, but they cannot close up shop since their plastrons are not hinged. You can easily identify the breed by its shell and its orange throat and orange undersides of its legs. (Muhlenberg's turtle looks similar, but it has less pronounced sculpturing in the shell and bears an orange blotch on each side of its head.

Muhlenberg's turtle is rare, protected, and illegal to keep.)

Wood turtles are protected in many states. Check that you can legally keep one in your state before you move it into your backyard. If you can keep one, feed it in water with any raw, non-spiced food, including meat, vegetables, and fruit.

Terrestrial Turtles

Design your terrestrial turtle habitat based on the species' native habitat. Generally, you will supply ample dry habitat but with a source of water. Gopher turtles (*Gopherus* spp.) do not make good pets and have quite specific habitat needs, being native desert dwellers.

The diamondback terrapin, with its knobby and highly sculptured shell, has been one of the most studied American turtles because of its popularity as a food turtle.

BOX TURTLE

Terrapene carolina (green to brown with rounded yellow markings on its shell and head) and *T. ornata* (brown shell with barred yellow markings on its shell and head) are the common box turtles found in the woods. Their hinged plastron allows them to close up tightly when threatened.

Easy keepers, they require ample ambling room, a shallow source of water, and hibernation provisions. While digging a pit to below the frost line is one hibernation option, box turtles can hibernate safely to zone 5 when supplied with a very thick pile of mulch or straw. Accomplished diggers, they can burrow out of enclosures that do not have fencing extending two feet into the ground. Like other turtles, they are also good climbers. Containment requires they not be able to escape over the fence, too.

They appreciate a varied diet of chopped raw or cooked beef, along with lettuce, bananas, apple, melons, strawberries, and mushrooms.

The most commonly kept terrestrial turtle is the calm, placid box turtle. Shown here is Terrepene ornata, *which ranges from the Mississippi River to the foothills of the Rockies. Its markings tend to be in a pattern of golden bars, while its cousin* T. carolina's *markings tend to be more rounded, often into curved, hieroglyphics.*

Boy or Girl?

If you keep only one turtle, its sex won't make any difference. However, if you keep more than one, you may wish to know if you might expect and plan for breeding baby turtles.

In most species of turtle, the males have longer and thicker tails than the females of the same species. This allows the male to wrap his tail around and under the edge of the female's shell when they mate. The male's anal opening is also farther from the base of the tail than the female's. This, too, aids in mating. In some species, notably the red-ear turtle, the males posses longer front claws to enable a secure grasp during breeding. A box turtle male usually has red eyes, while the female often has brown eyes. The underside of the turtle's shell also characterizes its sex. Males often have a shallow depression in their plastron, while the female's may be flat or actually bulging to provide more room for egg storage.

Breeding

Turtles form no lasting relationship between mates. A male finds a female who acts or smells right, and he rubs her face with his long claws, butts her with the front of his shell, or bites her legs. If she agrees, he climbs on her back and they mate.

A fertilized female may remain fertile for several years, but each successive clutch of eggs contains fewer fertile eggs. She wanders off to an isolated and seemingly safe place where she digs a hole in which to lay the eggs. A painted turtle may lay only five or six eggs, while a large snapping turtle may lay as many as 70 or 80 eggs.

Turtle eggs are always white, generally leathery, and often elliptical or spherical. Once the eggs have been laid, the female covers them with dirt. The young of smaller species generally hatch in two or three months. In northern climates, eggs laid in September may not hatch until the following May. If your pet turtle lays eggs, do not disturb them. You can store them, without handling them, in slightly dampened sand or living sphagnum moss in a dark place maintained at 75°F. They may or may not hatch. If they hatch, you will have babies within two or three months. As soon as the hatchlings emerge from their shells, they require water to drink.

Hatchlings are active at birth. The hatchling cuts through its eggshell with a tiny egg tooth located on its nose.

A pet red-ear turtle that wandered off into the backyard and found the koi pond also found food. This young koi shows signs of stress—it has clamped fins and is hyperventilating–caused by a turtle bite in the back.

This egg tooth soon falls off. Since the mother laid the eggs months before, burying them and leaving them, the hatchlings are on their own. No turtle takes care of its young. We have had enchanting summers when baby red-ears, no bigger than a quarter, could be spotted wandering around in the grass, about the driveway, and perched on lily pads in the ponds.

Stocking

Turtles in nature don't thrive in polluted waters. Don't crowd your animals. Begin turtle keeping with only one or two in a roomy habitat.

Companions for Turtles

1. Don't keep both terrestrial species and aquatic species in the same habitat. Terrestrial turtles develop fungus and/or pneumonia from excess moisture. Aquatic turtles may never be seen.

2. Consider natural dispositions. Snappers are predatory and will eat even smaller turtles. Snappers and soft-shell turtles are not good companions for even each other.

3. Wood turtles and same-size frogs can be together. Smaller frogs are food.

4. Bullfrogs and green frogs (*Rana*) should not be kept with

aquatics or with semiaquatic turtles. One or the other becomes somebody's dinner.

5. Diamondbacks may be kept together. None of the other semiaquatic turtles are suited to the diamondback's requirement of brackish water.

6. Snakes and lizards may be kept in similarly satisfying habitats with all but snappers and soft-shells.

7. Toads and terrestrial turtles are compatible.

8. Crocodiles, alligators, and caimans should not be kept with any turtles.

9. A few fish in an aquatic habitat are encouraged by most turtles. Most aquatic and semiaquatic turtles will view fish as food if you do not keep them sated.

10. Water boatmen and dragonflies are okay with aquatic turtles, although some will get eaten. Leeches are dangerous parasites.

11. Don't mix diurnal and nocturnal animals in small habitats—they will keep each other awake. Most land turtles are diurunal, while some aquatic turtles are not.

Creating an Outdoor Turtle Habitat

To accommodate the needs of any turtles, plan your turtle habitat to be at least three square feet, preferably much larger.

Turtles are climbers and turtles are diggers. If you want to be sure that your pet stays around, construct the habitat's enclosure both above and below ground. The minimum depth recommended for turtle fencing

Provide your terrestrial turtle pet with ample area offering both shade and sun. Be sure your enclosure fence is embedded deeply enough into the ground to prevent escape.

Even terrestrial turtles appreciate a very shallow pond for refreshment and drinking.

Use a reservoir hidden in the ground as the water source for a flowing fountain/waterfall to offer water to your terrestrial turtle.

is two feet into the ground. When you plan the enclosure's height, consider rocks that might be climbed in a break for freedom. Including an overhang on the fence will prevent all-American athletes from scaling the fence. Supply a similar overhang to waterfalls in their water features. They won't mind climbing a wet stairway if at the top they attain freedom.

Your habitat floor should include winter accommodations. Dig a pit to a depth below your frost line and heap it full of leaves, grass clippings, or loosened straw. Once your turtle has buried itself in its winter bed, do not disturb it or seek to alter the existing temperatures. Its system is in a very delicate state of balance, maintaining its body with stored food reserves. A hibernating turtle, if too cold, will freeze and die. A too-warm hibernating turtle remains slightly active with more heartbeats, breaths, and energy consumption, using stored food supplies in its body. It can then die of starvation before spring. All you can do during the winter is wait until your turtle awakens and lumbers from its hibernation bed in quest of food.

Even though all turtles need sunlight, provide a shady place in your outdoor turtle pen. Since turtles are cold-blooded animals and since they cannot internally regulate their temper-

A self-enclosed turtle pond habitat for the semiaquatic turtle provides extended rocks around the upper edge to prevent escape. Water fills the bottom level of the pond with basking rocks set on the planting shelf. A waterfall recycles the water.

ature, they must search out the degree of warmth that suits them. Aquatic turtles appreciate, and semiaquatic turtles *require,* a dry basking area out of the water. A sunny rock or piece of driftwood is welcomed in the mornings. The flat basking rock also provides a handy place for feeding where the turtles can readily take their food into the water to eat.

Reservoir Water Feature Construction

Use a whiskey barrel-size plastic container as your reservoir. Dig a hole deep enough to accommodate both the con-

tainer and a layer of rocks over it. After setting the container into its excavation, set in a small submersible pump (80- to 120-GPH size) with black plastic tubing long enough to reach the outlet of your water feature above. Fill the container with water, and fit a grate over the top. Cover the grate with cobblestones or gravel large enough not to fall through. Set up your water feature so water can flow through it and into the rocks covering the grate. Connect the tubing from the submersible pump to the water feature. Plug it in and let it run. Top off your reservoir container every week or two. The water will remain cool even during hot weather.

Preformed Turtle Ponds

Using a preformed pond shell simplifies construction of your turtle pond. Simply follow the directions given in Chapter 2 for installation of a preformed pond in the ground. You can also set up your preformed pond aboveground, but be sure to provide adequate support to the side walls to prevent buckling and cracking.

Preformed ponds are especially suited to keeping turtles as they usually have built-in planting shelves about halfway up the pond's depth. This allows you to keep the lower portion filled with water and set up with access ramps of wood or flat stones to the shelf. If the water reaches onto the pond's shelf, provide additional flat stones for sunning and drying. You can also provide floating islands on which the turtles may sun themselves. The tropical *Neptunia*, the water sensitive plant, offers a thick, buoyant, floating rootstock that offers small turtles respite from the water.

Use a submersible pump affixed with a mechanical filter to prevent sediment from circulating through the pump. Also provide adequate mechanical filtration to the water before it is returned to the pond.

Seeding the pond with the

Another form of the self-enclosed turtle pond is a liner construction enclosed within an aboveground, wood frame. Driftwood and floating Neptunia provide cover and basking opportunity for the diamondback terrapins inside. Water is recycled through a separate vegetable filter filled with hydroponically grown water celery (Oenanthe).

"sludge-eating" bacteria *Bacillus subtilis* may aid in keeping the pond clean and healthy, but do not rely on it in lieu of regular pond cleanings. Avoid extensive use of gravel in the bottom of the pond as your cleaning then becomes more labor intensive. Gravel used on the bottom accumulates organic settlement without notice, lulling the turtle keeper into a false sense of pond cleanliness. Remember that accumulations of feces invite Salmonella. A clean pond is important for both your health and that of your turtle.

Your turtle pond can be set up in your sunroom, too. You do not need to provide hibernation facilities for the turtle kept indoors through the winter. Do provide extra light and warmth, if necessary, so the days remain comparable to summer days. Remember that turtles need sunlight; even during the summertime provide the light to the quarters kept indoors. You can heat the water in your turtle tank with an aquarium heater. Terrestrial setups are heated with under-tank heating pads or dry heaters.

How deep should you keep the water? Even for aquatic turtles, the water need be no deeper than that required to fully cover the shell. However, turtles will appreciate enough depth to allow some swimming exercise as well as the opportunity to find hiding places under water. The water's area should be at least three times the size of your turtle. Turtles appreciate as much room as you can possibly provide.

A liner pond can also be constructed using the same procedure described in chapter two. However, include shallow shelves in your excavation/con-

Provide variety in your turtle's diet to assure that its nutritional needs are met. This box turtle (Terrepene carolina) *enjoys strawberries, grapes, and melon.*

struction and complete the pond suited to your turtle's needs, providing rocks emerging from the water within the pond, as well as supplying flat, accessible edging rocks.

Feeding Your Turtle

Like that of a fish, a turtle's digestion is temperature-dependent. Feeding a turtle and then allowing it to become chilled can result in the turtle's death. Feed your turtles only when the temperature ranges from 65 to 96°F. (Feed very

lightly in the range from 65 to 75°F, and adjust feeding to suit your pet.)

Aquatic and semiaquatic species eat underwater. Of the turtles discussed in this chapter, only the box turtle eats outside the water. You may either toss their food into the water or set it upon a flat rock from which the turtle can pull the food into the water for eating. Generally, during warm weather, a turtle eats a volume of food equal to half the size of its head every day. Most will eat more if you offer it. They will survive on less food, however perhaps not in as good health as with more. Particularly voracious feeders such as the snapper will eat much more.

Semiaquatic turtles (red-ears and painteds) prefer fresh fish, frogs, birds, carrion, worms, snails, and crawfish. They also enjoy crickets, fish, liver, earthworms, lean beef, and even canned dog food. The freeze-dried tubifex worms stocked in pet stores for fish are also appreciated. Turtles will eat plants if animal food is not available. Aquatic turtles, however, will eat plants only when they are very hungry. Test your turtle's interest in vegetables with lettuce. If it partakes, try other vegetables, too. Most turtles enjoy "dessert," too. Provide halved grapes, whole strawberries, or chunks of melon. Whatever the food you feed, it should be low in fat. Turtles cannot digest fatty foods.

Turtle Health

A healthy turtle has bright, clear eyes with no milky cast to them. The turtle is strong and plump. If the turtle is so fat as not to be able to withdraw into its shell, a healthy turtle still displays strength. (A fat turtle may simply be a female ready to lay eggs!) Its shell is not cracked, its tail is normal-

appearing, and there are no open sores on its limbs, head, or tail. The mouth and throat display no evidence of fungus or strange-looking material.

Bright, clear eyes are a sign of good health in a turtle.

Health Problems

Minor Injuries: Provide clean quarters with a place for sunning in direct sunlight. A 3 to $3\frac{1}{2}$ percent concentration salt bath for up to an hour only once in any 24-hour period may aid healing and prevent infection. Cauterize open abrasions with seven percent tincture of iodine. Treat minor wound infections with Neosporin or Panalog. Use a fungicide ointment with fungal infections.

Shell Rot: Provide clean quarters and a place for basking in direct sunlight. Clean affected shell portions and treat

with seven percent tincture of iodine.

Soft Shell: A hard-shelled turtle experiencing soft shell growth is suffering from a calcium deficiency. Feed whole fish (with bones) to compensate for this, along with Vitamin D to enable the turtle's body to absorb the calcium. Simply providing direct sunlight can help, too. Vitamin D is blocked by window glass, so use dietary supplements for the turtle housed indoors or under glass.

Swollen or Pop-Eyes: This usually indicates an incurable problem, often nutritional. If the eyes are popping, it is probably too late to save the pet.

Be sure the pet has clean quarters and feed a balanced diet.

Ticks or Leeches: Wipe the offending parasite with rubbing alcohol and pluck it away with tweezers. Red-ear turtles and diamondback terrapins can be dipped in a three percent salt solution, as are fish. (See Chapter 5.)

Worms: Worms, particularly roundworms in the feces, are treated by your veterinarian. Remove all fecal matter immediately and provide clean quarters.

Bird Ponds

*A dripper or a mister added to the side of a shallow, rock-accented basin will give
a real treat to any birds that visit your garden.*

New pond owners are delighted to discover that adding a pond, waterfall, or stream invites birds to the garden landscape–often birds not seen before in the backyard. Some pond-keepers actually design their water garden with a shallow, pebbled beach especially for bird guests. However, if fish are kept in the waters visited by birds, they are at risk. Birds are the vector for parasites that prey on fish. The life cycle of the anchor worm, for example, involves introduction into the pond by birds. The parasite may be harbored in snails as the intermediary host, and then the female worms attach themselves to your fish. You can interrupt this life cycle by keeping the pond scrupulously free of snails…or you can accommodate both the fish and the birds by giving the birds their own water features for drinking and bathing.

Water gardeners who construct streams as part of their pond system soon discover its attractiveness to neighborhood birds.

Creating a Bird Pond Habitat

Birds readily drink from water features that offer easy access from nearby branches or rocks framing water. To encourage their bathing, offer them sure footing in the pond with a sand or gravel bottom. Using sand or gravel also provides a lighter-colored bottom to the feature than that provided by black pond liners. Birds need to see that the water is shallow enough for bathing. Even when bathing, their feet remain firmly on the bottom. Three inches of water is considered the maximum depth in which they will bathe. Since artificially constructed streams usually run within this depth range, keeping the water flow very gentle entices many to bathe. However, according to Bill Fintel, as long as the water level is shallow, birds will still bathe in water moving one half foot per second. With a few cobbles tucked into the stream, you can then enjoy the sound of a babbling brook.

Your birds' pond or stream should offer a sense of security. Siting it within an area open on at least one side allows the birds to feel safe from predators, such as neighborhood cats, that might lurk among nearby plants. (Outfitting your cat with a bell lends extra protection, too.) While the water feature itself may be in the open, you'll still want to provide a nearby shrub where the birds may perch and preen after their dips. Supplying a branch over a portion of the water feature provides what Bill Fintel calls an "inspection perch." New visitors like to check out the terrain before indulging with abandon.

If you've kept a birdbath, you know that stagnant, shallow reservoirs of water accumulate scummy green and red algae coatings. These may be controlled with weekly brush scrubbings. Mosquitoes also breed in them. Having the water move through your bird's water feature prevents mosquito breeding.

Setting up the feature in the shade helps prevent algae growth. If you would set the feature in the sunlight, you can run it from a hidden reservoir

that shades the water source. A whiskey barrel-size reservoir adequately services a birdbath. As in the water garden, using plants within the bird feature also helps control algae. Fintel recommends 15 to 25 percent of the bird pond's surface be devoted to such plants. Do not use chemicals within the bird's water!

Siting the Birds' Water Feature

Pick a site for your birds' water feature where you can easily watch it, usually within 20 to 40 feet from your home. If you select a site to the east or north of your bird-watching

window, you'll enjoy better afternoon viewing.

Avoid sites that normally collect standing water or that lie in the course of surface runoff. Not only can toxic lawn chemicals be washed into the bird's water, but muddy water can as well, necessitating increased maintenance.

A nearby shrub or a small tree provides perching and preening areas, but too much ground cover is disconcerting to the birds' sense of safety. Allow at least one side of the feature to be open. If landscape plants are not available at the site, plant hummingbird-attractive perennials and annuals along one side of the feature. (See page 139.) This can be as

The mere presence of water, the attractive Avian Dripper, and the obviously shallow water within an open site ensure visits by birds to your backyard. Photo courtesy of Avian Aquatics

simple as pots of geraniums and petunias. Provide a perch with a long branch.

You may wish to make your bird pond part of a dedicated bird area in your garden. Site the pond near your primary feeding stations, but not so close that birdseed and hulls fall into the pond to complicate cleaning and maintenance. If you have the space, include a bird meadow of seed-bearing grasses and native flowers where the birds can find natural sources of food, too.

The Hidden Reservoir

Hidden or buried reservoirs are often used by water gardeners to create child-safe stream gardens and to set up flowing water ornaments. They are also a practical way of supplying a water source to bird features. The beauty of the reservoir water feature is that water remains cool even in hot climates, as the water source is both shaded and insulated.

Reservoir Construction

Select your site and dig a hole deep enough to accommodate your reservoir container. At the bottom of the container, set a

A millstone with water gently overflowing into the hidden reservoir below attracts birds to drink and bathe. Photo by Charles A. Henne

A hidden reservoir recycles water onto a concave rock surface and provides a drinking source for birds. The water overflows and returns to the reservoir hidden below the surrounding rocks.

small submersible pump. Pumps sized to move 80 to 150 gallons per hour are usually sufficient. Affix enough tubing to the pump so the water can be directed to a spouting ornament or an inflow point of the water feature. Fit a heavy-duty plastic, fiberglass, or stainless steel grate over the top of the container, bringing the water line up through it to await its outlet connection. Fill the container with water.

Cover the grate with cobbles or stones large enough not to slip through the grate. If you wish to use small gravel such as pea gravel or even aquarium gravel, rig up a plastic or fiberglass screen tray for the fine gravel. Screening is available by the yard from home and building supply stores. Use pieces of wood to form your frame, stapling the screen to it. Camouflage the upturned edge of your screen-tray with cobbles. Accessing your reservoir's grate cover is then simply a matter of removing the screen tray. This may facilitate cleaning, too.

Set up your water feature over the grate so water overflows into the cobbles over the reservoir. In operation, water is kept cool and dark in the reservoir as it is directed up through the water feature and flows back into the reservoir. Birdbaths, small streams, overflowing decorative jars, and millstones are some of the options you can use with this construction method.

Reservoir System Maintenance

When first setting up a reservoir system, monitor evaporation rate as reflected by the level of water maintained in the reservoir. Once you know how many weeks it takes for the water to drop a few inches, you can plan to top off your reservoir regularly, filling it with a

hose directly through the gravel/rocks over the grate cover.

Particulate matter may wash down through the rocks and into the reservoir. If your pump is set up from the bottom by a couple inches, you will not risk pulling the particulates through the pump. A mechanical filter attached to the intake of the pump will also prevent particulate circulation. Once every month or two, pull back the rocks, lift the grate, and lower the water with the submersible pump so that only a couple inches of water remain in the bottom. Use a shop vac to remove the remaining water and the settlement solids within. Your water supply then remains fresh and clean.

Even in zones 4 and 5, you can keep your reservoir system running all winter long without the benefit of a heater. If a heater is necessary, affix it to the unit so you can supply water to the birds throughout the winter. Clean the system in the fall and again in the spring, resuming your monthly cleaning during the summer.

Bird Ponds

As long as one side of the pond is kept open, birds tend to prefer in-ground ponds to elevated birdbaths. Bird ponds need be only one to three inches

deep. Minimal excavation is required. If your bird pond will be large enough, you may wish to excavate a sump area in the center for a small submersible pump. The pump can recycle water through a waterfall/ stream or a bird-attractive fountain and be used to drain the pond for cleaning. The very shallow pond can be emptied and cleaned with a shop vac, too.

You can construct a bird pond with scraps from your lined fish pond, but the smooth surface will be slippery. A light layer of sand or pea gravel allows the birds to see that the depth is suited for bathing, and allows them to feel more secure in the water. The bottom should be level for sure footing.

You will need to clean the pond periodically, so keep in mind that using loose gravel or sand will create more maintenance problems. The easiest way to clean a shallow bird pond, of course, is to simply sweep it clean. If you construct your gravel-lined bird pond within a surround of such gravel, you can sweep the pond clean and then move the gravel back into the pond. Frame the total area with larger stones, bricks, or blocks to confine the gravel.

Setting a few flat rocks to extend above the water within the pond, as well as around the edges, provides access to the water. A tree branch also pro-vides access and perching. If you do not keep water flowing through the pond, you will need to empty, scrub, and refill the pond every week or two to keep the water fresh and healthy for the birds.

Bird-Pond Kits

In 1990 Bill Fintel formed a small company devoted to pro-ducing water products and information to enable people to attract and offer sanctuary to a wide variety of songbirds and other wildlife. Concerned with the steadily increasing loss of natural habitat, his company, Avian Aquatics of Harbeson, Delaware, contributes a portion of its sales revenue to conserva-tion organizations dedicated to preserving natural areas, espe-cially tropical rain forests.

Avian Aquatics has devel-oped a wide variety of bird ponds and water features. Free-form birdbath pond kits come in 2 × 3-foot, 3 × 5 -foot, and 4 × 6-foot sizes; the liners are either 20-mil or 40-mil thick, black synthetic rubber, Avaqlon, that bears a textured surface for sure footing and algae resistance. The 40-mil liner is recommended for rocky soil and for sites where large animals such as deer might walk. Bird-Creek recirculating bird ponds imitate a shallow

The rocks surrounding the Avian Dripper provide birds both access to the water and visual confirmation of its accessibility. Photo courtesy of Avian Aquatics

mountain brook with one to two inches of water flowing gently over a gravel creek bottom. The beauty of these kits is their completeness. Liner, pump, tubing and connectors,

Waterfall Flowmaster or Avian Dripper, beneficial bacteria, and waterfall bib are all pro-vided. You need only supply the gravel, water, and any plants you might wish to enhance the

Set up your bird feeders in the same area as your bird-attractive water feature, but site feeders so seeds do not drop into the water.

bird pond. The designs include single pools, tiered pools, and cascading pools.

Avian Aquatics offers a series of bird streams, too. These stream designs use a gravel-bed biological filter that is enhanced with bacterial-enzyme concentrate provided with the kits to accelerate implementation of the nitrifying bacteria. Remember that the nitrogen cycle occurs with decomposing organic matter, such as bird droppings, as well as with the direct addition of ammonia to the water through fish metabolism. A small pump is buried within the shallow gravel layer so water flows down through the gravel for recycling, much like the under-gravel system used in aquariums. Water is oxygenated as it flows through the system with additional aeration supplied by the waterfall.

Planting directly into the gravel of the stream bed allows plants to help with nitrate removal from the water. Besides the aquatic plants listed on pages 89–90, Bill Fintel reports growing hostas and impatiens successfully in the shallow stream beds. Prune plants to keep their growth under control and allow enough bathing room for the birds.

Fintel notes that normally occurring mossy algae on the gravel substrate is alleviated by the birds themselves as their feet roll the gravel and wear off algae growth.

Moving the Water

Using a pump provides cleaner and healthier water. You have several ways to present the moving water to the birds. Waterfall Flowmasters, an exclusive design from Avian Aquatics, are designed to spread the water from the pump out into a four-inch-wide gurgling curtain of water. Tubing from the pump is connected to the back of the Flowmaster, and the Flowmaster is set on top of your other waterfall rocks with one more flat rock set on top to hide the tubing. A low-profile design made of concrete, the Flowmaster works well up to 700 gallons per hour. With a natural appearance, the preform waterfall allows you to avoid water loss common to traditional stacked-rock constructions.

The Avian Dripper appeals to birds because of the gentle ripples it creates in a birdbath. Often the birds perch on the dripper itself to drink directly from the end of the tube. A dripper is a valued bird accessory where water conservation is critical, because flow rates can be adjusted down to one pint per hour with a noncorroding PVC-regulating valve.

Misters that create soft, fine sprays of water are highly attractive to birds. They can be used in conjunction with a birdbath or pond, or they can be set up within a shrub or tree to function as a leaf-mister, which is especially attractive to hummingbirds.

The Rock-Mister can be placed in both ground-level and pedestal birdbaths to attract songbirds. It comes complete with a low-flow mist nozzle, 100-mesh filter, regulating valve, rock base or pebble base, 60 feet of small black tubing, necessary connectors, and a Y valve that allows the garden hose and mister to be used at the same time.

The hummingbird's favorite is the Leaf-Mister. The mist nozzle is attached to a low limb and is aimed in the direction of easily viewed foliage. The tubing is run back to an outdoor faucet and connected with the Y valve. In cooler weather, you can convert the mister to a dripper by removing the mist nozzle and adjusting the regulating valve so that water drips from the end of the tubing. It comes complete with a low-flow mist nozzle, 100-mesh filter, regulating valve, 60 feet of small black tubing, the necessary connectors, and a Y valve to allow use of both garden hose and mister at the same time.

Birds and Winter

While fish ponds tend to slumber throughout the winter, bird ponds and similar water sources require tending throughout the winter months.

De-icers may be critical to your neighborhood birds' winter survival. Especially when other water sources remain frozen for several days or weeks at a time, birds may depend on you for their very lives. The following bird de-icers are manufactured by Farm Innovators and are representative of products available in the marketplace. Bill Fintel prefers the C-250 model because of the 6-foot cord not offered with most other de-icers.

B-9 De-icer. A 44-watt non-thermostatic de-icer, the B-9 de-icer can be used under thin-walled birdbaths. With the heating element laminated between foil, it is safe for use in plastic birdbaths. While it comes with an 8-inch electric cord, you can also buy it as a do-it-yourself kit that contains foam insulation and two cord clips.

C-50 De-Icer. A doughnut-shaped 50-watt thermostatic unit that is made of cast aluminum comes with a one-foot cord and is safe for use in plastic baths. The integral thermostat prevents overheating. CSA approved.

C-250 De-Icer. This 250-watt thermostatic de-icer is recommended for recirculating baths with a water surface greater than three square feet. It is also recommended for baths where temperatures fall below 5°F. In tests in Minnesota, this de-icer maintained open water down to –20°F in a 300-square-foot bird pond. Made of doughnut-shaped cast aluminum, it comes with an integral thermostat and a 6-foot electric cord.

Thermostat Plug. An ingenious and unique device turns your de-icer into an automatic unit that turns on when temperatures fall below 35°F and turns off when the temperature rises above 45°F may be used with thermostatically controlled de-icers to help conserve energy.

If you do not have feeders set up near your birds' water feature, you will probably want to put them out in the winter so you can offer both food and water. Remember that birds need grit with their food, so including a sandy, dry beach area near the pond and feeders will be appreciated.

Electricity and Pumps

Obviously, birds are attracted to the simple presence of water in the garden. However, the attraction increases when the water is in motion, whether through a waterfall, a fountain, a dripper, or a mister. Moving water is healthier water, too. Mosquitoes do not breed in moving water, and the water contains more dissolved oxygen. To move water, you will need electricity. Be sure any electrical appliance used outdoors is connected to a GFCI outlet. If you do not have one, you can purchase a portable GFCI that plugs into an unprotected outdoor outlet. Connecting your pump or de-icer to the outlet socket of the GFCI then provides protection.

The chart below gives you an idea of the sizes and capabilities of some of the many pump choices. Bill Fintel suggests that

Pump and Waterfall Chart

The table below gives basic guidelines for selecting a pump for the water feature for your bird pond. Avian Aquatics makes the following recommendations: Be sure the pump you select will fit in your water feature and provide 40 to 60 gallons per hour (GPH) per inch of the width of the waterfall.

Water Feature	Pump Manufacturer	Model #	Pump Type	Watts	UL/CSA	Cord Length	Avian Aquatics Test		GPH*
							1' elev 2' of 1/2"	3 ft elev 15' of 3/4"	shutoff hgt
small fountain	CAL pump	P80	mag drive	5	yes	6'	60		2 ft
	RIO	180	mag drive	3	pending	6'	80		3 ft
large fountain	CAL Pump	P140	mag drive	10	yes	6'	120		5 ft
	RIO	600	mag drive	9	pending	6'	160		4 ft
3x5' to 5x6' pond	Little Giant	PE-1F-WG	direct drive	36	yes	15		170	7 ft
	Pondmaster (R)	PT250	mag drive	24	yes	10'		170	7 ft
5x6' to 8x12' pond	RIO	2100	mag drive	25	pending	15'		265	8 ft

Avian Aquatics test data provides GPH for each pump on the same basis of discharge elevation, hose length, and hose ID. Chart courtesy of Avian Aquatics

in choosing a pump it is important to consider the flow rate at the lift height (usually the top of the waterfall), 40 to 60 gallons per hour per inch of waterfall spillway being the minimum size.

In selecting a pump, consider the cost of operation, since you will run it around the clock and throughout the year. Magnetic drive pumps are available in both submersible and external models. The smaller models involved in operating bird ponds usually cost a few cents less a day to operate than traditional oil-encapsulated, submersible pumps. You can figure how much the pump costs to operate by knowing how much your electric company charges for wattage use. Compare that with the wattage required for any given pump. Many pump companies and retailers provide this information.

Enhance Your Backyard Habitat for the Birds

Avian Aquatics suggests the following to enhance your backyard habitat:

* Plant evergreens for roosting, nesting, and cover from predators.
* Plant varieties of flowers that hummingbirds like, such as *Lobelia cardinalis* (cardinal flower) that can be grown in ponds.
* Plant fruit trees and shrubs to provide food for non-seed-eating birds like waxwings.
* Leave tall trees, particularly oaks and hickories, for upper canopy foragers such as tanagers and orioles.
* Do not use pesticides in your yard; leave grubs and insects for robins, flickers, and other birds.
* Allow flowers to go to seed for juncos, sparrows, and finches.
* Leave dead wood, both limbs and trees, for woodpeckers to use as nesting cavities and to feed on.
* Use plants native to your region. They will usually thrive better, provide a more natural habitat, and provide food for indigenous species.
* Vary the types of plant to create a more diverse micro-habitat to attract a wider variety of birds and other wildlife.
* Install water sources so they will become an integral part of your landscape, i.e., plant moisture-loving plants like lobelia near your misters.

Attracting Hummingbirds to Your Garden

As our koi or water lilies are the jewels of our pools, so are hummingbirds the jewels of our gardens. These tiny, four-inch birds have the remarkable capacity to fly backward and hover in place with wing beats so rapid they make a humming sound.

The ruby-throated hummingbird is a delightful garden visitor treasured by many backyard gardeners. Photo by Perry D. Slocum

When hummingbirds return in the spring, they seem to follow the blooming of red-flowered plants. Many bird-watchers set out their hummingbird feeders when the red quince begins to bloom. In the Northeast, birders look for the first hummingbirds in mid-April when the azaleas begin to bloom.

Providing sugar water attracts these darlings to your yard, but it takes more to keep them from leaving. Their primary foods are spiders and other small insects, along with flower nectars that supply more nutrition than straight sugar water. Planting flowers that provide summerlong meals encourages them to frequent your backyard haven. Providing thickets of shrubs and small trees gives them shelter and sites for perching and nesting.

Don't forget to include hummingbird-attractive plants within your pond. Just as the terrestrial species of *Lobelia*, with their tube-shaped flowers, prove enticing, so will the aquatic *Lobelia cardinalis*, the cardinal flower. This plant blooms midsummer until fall and provides nourishment during the breeding season. Remember, too, that the terrestrial *Lobelia* can be adapted to water culture! The native marginal aquatic, *Mimulus* or monkey flower, also attracts

hummers. While most of the species and varieties are annuals in most of the U.S., you may be able to locate some of the more brightly colored forms that will please both the birds and yourself. (These plants reseed readily to make seed collection for the next year part of your summer regimen.) Water mint, *Mentha aquatica*, provides charming lavender flowers to attract hummers to your pond, too. In the bog garden or along a stream, plant turtlehead, *Chelone*, to feed your hummers. And don't forget *Lythrum*, if it is legal in your state.

Consult the hummingbird lists below to select enticing plants for your Earth-friendly garden. After all, there's not much better in the world than sitting in your own private haven and enjoying fish and flowers in your pond while hummingbirds zip around you. Don't forget to supply the hummingbirds with a mister among your plantings, too, so they can bathe and drink at their private banquet table, your backyard.

Plants to Attract Hummingbirds

In the following list of plants, "A" stands for annual and "B" for biennial; the perennial hardiness zones are as noted in *The American Horticultural Society*

A–Z Encyclopedia of Garden Plants. A single asterisk indicates moisture-loving but well-drained plants. A double asterisk indicates plants that

Lobelia cardinalis, *commonly called the cardinal flower, grows in your garden pond or in moist soils to attract and feed hummingbirds in midsummer.*

will grow in wet soils such as within a pond or in stream shallows or in a damp/bog garden. Note that many of these plants are native species.

Achillea, Yarrow (4–10)

Asclepias, Butterfly weed (3–9)**

Agastache, Hyssop (4–10)

Ageratum houstonianum, Ageratum (A)*

Althea or *Alcea*, Hollyhock (3–9)

Apocynum spp., Dogbane (4–9)

Aquilegia, Columbine (3–10)

Aster novae-angliae, New England aster (3–8)

Astilbe × arendsii, Astilbe (3–9)*

Belamcanda chinensis, Leopard lily (4–10)

Bidens aristosa, Tickseed sunflower (A)*

Bignonia capreolata, Cross vine, Trumpet flower (6–10)

Buddleia davidii, Butterfly bush (5–9)

Campsis radicans, Trumpet vine (5–9)

Chelone, Turtlehead (4–9)**

Cleome hasslerana, Cleome (A)

Coreopsis lanceolata, Lance-leaved coreopsis (3–8)

Cornus canadensis, Bunchberry (2–7)*

Cosmos spp., Cosmos (A)*

Daucus carota var. 'Carota', Queen Anne's lace (B; 5–10)

Delphinium, Delphinium (3–10)

Echinacea purpurea, Purple coneflower (4–8)*

Echinops ritro, Globe thistle (3–8)

Epilobium angustifolium, Fireweed (3–7)

Erythronium americanum, Yellow trout lily (3–8)*

Fragaria virginiana, Wild strawberry (5–10)

Fuchsia spp., Fuchsia (A; 8–10)

Gaultheria hispidula, Creeping snowberry*

Gaultheria procumbens, Wintergreen or Teaberry (4–8)*

Helenium autumnale, Sneezeweed (3–8)

Helianthus annus, Common sunflower (A)

Heliotropium arborescens, Heliotrope (A)

Heuchera, Coral bell (3–10)

Impatiens wallerana, Impatiens (A; 9–10)

Ipomoea quamoclit, Cardinal climber, Cypress vine (8–10)

Kniphofia uvaria, Red-hot poker (5–9)

Lobelia cardinalis, Cardinal flower (2–9)**

Lobelia spp., Lobelia, Cardinal flower (4–9)**

Lonicera sempervirens, Trumpet honeysuckle (4–9)

Lupinus spp., Lupine (5–9)

Mahonia repens, Creeping mahonia (4–7)

Mandevilla splendens, Mandevilla (A; 9–10)

Mentha spp., Mint (4–9)

Mentha aquatica, Water mint (4–9)**

Mimulus cardinalis, Scarlet monkey flower (A; 9–11)**

Mirabilis jalapa, Four-o'clock (A; 9–10)

Mitchella repens, Partridgeberry (4–9)*

Monarda didyma, Bee balm (4–10)

Nasturtium, Tropaeolum (A)

Nepeta, Catmint (3–10)

Nicotiana, Nicotiana (A)

Oenothera, Evening primrose, Sundrop (3–9)

Pelargonia × hortorum, Geranium (A; 9–10)

Pelargonium, Scented geranium (A; 9–10)

Penstemon, Penstemon (3–9)

Petunia spp., Petunia (A)

Phlox paniculata, Phlox (3–9)

Solidago, Goldenrod (3–9)

Rudbeckia fulgida, Black-eyed Susan (3–9)*

Salvia elegans, Pineapple sage (A; 8–10)

Salvia coccinea, Salvias (A; 8–10)

Sedum spectabile, Showy sedum (3–9)

Tithonia rotundifolia, Tithonia (A)

Trifolium pratense, Red clover (4–9)

Verbena spp., Verbena (A; 9–10 or 4–10)

Veronia noveboracensis, Ironweed (5–10)**

Vitis gulpina, Fox grape (5–9)

Zauschneria californica, Hummingbird flower (A; 8–10)

Zinnia elegans, Zinnia (A)

Shrubs and Trees Attractive to Hummingbirds

Callistemon citrinus 'Splendens', Lemon bottle-brush (8–10)*

Chaenomeles speciosa, Flowering quince (5–9)

Cornus florida, Flowering dogwood (5–9)*

Cornus sericea, Red-osier dogwood (3–8)*

Fuchsia boliviana or *F. brustus*, (4–10)*
Ilex verticillata, Winterberry (4–9)
Justicia brandegeano, Shrimp plant (A; 8–10)
Malus spp., Wild crabapple (3–8)*
Morus rubra, Red mulberry (5–9)*
Myrica cerifera, Wax myrtle or Bayberry (8–9)*
Myrica pensylvanica, Bayberry (3–6)
Ocotillo, 8–10
Prunus pensylvanica, Pin cherry (3–8)
Prunus virginiana, Chokecherry, Virginia bird cherry (3–8)*
Pyracantha coccinea, Scarlet firethorn (6–9)

Rhododendron spp., Rhododendron, Azalea (5–9)
Rhus typhina, Staghorn sumac (3–8)
Rosa rugosa, Rugosa rose (2–7)
Rubus allegheniensis, Common blackberry (5–9)
Sambucus canadensis, American elderberry (4–9)*
Syringa 'Belle de Nancy' and 'Souvenir de Louis Spath', Lilac (4–8)
Viburnum trilobum, American cranberrybush (4–9)*
Viburnum dentatum, Arrowwood virburnum (4–9)*

CHAPTER EIGHT

Other Life Attracted to the Garden Pond

A male Louisiana heron performs his mating ritual, but a prelude to more herons visiting your pond! Photo by Ron Everhart

Building a pond for the special pets that you will keep in it is only the first step in creating what evolves into a backyard habitat for yourself and the Earth. An Earth-friendly pond functions healthily for its water inhabitants as well as functioning as a closely interrelated part of the rest of the environment. Although you may begin with a pond for special fish and plants, you will soon begin tailoring the pond and the rest of your garden to take into account the needs of the other lives attracted to your personal haven.

Predators

Bearing in mind that ponds attract wildlife, first consider how to protect the life within the pond. Regional areas may find less common predators visiting the pond, such as muskrats, otters, or even alligators. The deterrents suggested below will work for other species that visit the pond, too.

Egrets, Herons, and Other Predatory Birds

Many of these species are protected. This means that a shotgun is not the remedy to protect your fish. Living near a heron rookery, we've had to deal with these incredible birds on a daily basis, all year round. The belted kingfisher visits only during the height of the pond season–summer–and announces his arrival with an arrogant clatter. Other predatory birds are ospreys and crows.

There are many myths about herons that lead to ineffective protection of pond fish. Probably the most commonly heard is that herons are solitary feeders. This means that by placing a decoy of a heron or an egret by the pond, a bird flying overhead will see it and not stop to feed since there is already one feeding there. *This is true during the nonbreeding season.* During the breeding

During the summer months, using a decoy statue to dissuade herons is really more like erecting a neon sign that announces, "Eat here!"

Kit Knotts of Cocoa Beach, Florida, keeps fish basket-traps in the ponds to feed Fred, a green heron who knows a good thing when he finds it.

season, when herons are raising a nest of young, the adults range for food within only a limited distance of the nest. This cuts down on the number of sources of food, and herons are forced to feed together. The time of year when young are fed coincides with the height of the pond season–summer. I have watched three and four herons feed together in our summer ponds. Setting out a lifelike decoy then announces to any herons flying overhead that there is food within your small body of backyard water.

Another myth is that herons land and then walk to the water's edge. Believing this, people erect a fishing line six inches above the ground level as a barrier to the approaching heron. This method may work in some cases, as will dense landscaping. *However, herons will land in shallow waters to fish.* Ten percent of the time they will even hover above the water to fish. If you keep your pond water good and green (pea-soup algae!), the birds cannot see the shallow depth and will not land in the pond. Being inquisitive and aesthetic souls, however, we strive to keep our water clear. The herons easily see that the water is shallow enough to land in, and the hunt begins. The barrier fence stands useless around the pond.

Other common deterrents involve setting out a scarecrow or using a motion-detector device that sprays water at unwelcome visitors. Both may work on occasional visits. A persistent heron may figure out that the scarecrow doesn't move or that the startling spray of water is just water. You will find it more effective if you move the scarecrow or motion-detector every few days. Even keeping a dog or two in the yard may not help. One day I watched our six golden retrievers herding the fish from one side of the pond to the patient heron fishing on the other side, less than 20 feet away! Do not underestimate the intelligence of herons, and do not discount their biological instincts to feed both them-selves and their young.

The only way I know to fully protect pond fish from herons is to erect a shelter over-head or to net the pond. In southern states, where a full day's sunlight may be too much for many blooming aquatic plants, a lattice-style pergola protects the fish as well as lush growth of the plants. If you are not interested in growing blooming aquatic plants, or if your pond is strictly for fish, a shadecloth barrier or full roof works well. Small ponds can be draped with bird netting in a tentlike construction, much like mosquito netting over a tropical bed. One such treatment I saw in Florida involved white nylon fish net with lead weights on its edge. It was set up as a tent over the pond; the effect was quite lovely. A non-conspicuous netting over the pond that allows plant growth through it is clear fishing line strung in a crisscross grid over the entire pond surface. The grid, six to twelve inches square, is erected four to six inches above the pond's edge. Do not become complacent with this usually foolproof protection. Hungry herons will fish from planks used to support netting over a pond!

Raccoons

One summer when I was young, my uncle brought home two baby, orphaned raccoons. We raised them in our house. They were precious, much like kittens. As a pondkeeper, my

Raccoons are adorable to look at but deadly to your finned pets. Photo by Ron Everhart

feelings for these critters have changed. One of our ponds, home of fantail goldfish and black moors, was left with only one fish after a nighttime raid by raccoons. We tried chicken wire mesh over the pond. It was too lightweight to keep out the marauders. Mechanic's wire mesh worked, but it is not the most aesthetic solution.

The key to preventing raccoons from eating your fish is to construct the pond to make their efforts all but impossible. This involves *no* planting shelves (we call them "launching pads") and fairly steep-sided construction to the two-foot depth. Keeping the water a few inches below the pond edge also makes it more difficult for fishing. Planting water lilies near the edge of the pond provides additional protective cover for your fish. Because we are in the country and raccoons are numerous, we trained our fish to feed in the center of the pond. Ordinarily, fish trained to eat near the pond's edge will come up upon the vibration of a footstep. Training to feed in the pond's center allows them to spot pondside predators.

Even the best raccoon-proof construction may not deter the unwanted guests. Live traps, of course, are a humane option. Do not feed raccoons. They carry rabies and are a health risk to the hands that

would feed them. An electric wire erected around the perimeter of the pond's presents safety concerns and must be turned on and off as needed. Three other methods have been used around the U.S. with success:

*Suspend fox-urine–soaked rags (or tampons) around the pond's perimeter. (Effective, but perhaps not the method of choice for an outside dinner party.)

*Tuck a few mothballs among the landscaping and rocks every foot or so around the pond's perimeter. (But not so close to one another that you risk dropping them into the water and dissolving to risk your fish.)

*Bob Bon Giorno of Suburban Water Gardens in Dix Hills, New York, reports an interesting method that proves successful within two visits by raccoons. Cover round (and very hot) habanero peppers with peanut butter. (The raccoon who tries a second bite is a rare one indeed!)

Frogs

Remember the line in the film *Field of Dreams,* "If you build it, they will come"?

Those of us fortunate enough to live near bodies of water, be they lakes, rivers, creeks, ponds, or swampy wet-

lands, often find frogs showing up for the mating ritual. Each species has its own call. Living in the country, we have counted the calls of nine different frogs and toads breeding in our ponds. The spring peeper sounds like a forlorn and hungry baby bird chirping away into the night. This tiny frog is smaller even than the tree frog. Cricket and chorus

If your backyard pond is located anywhere near a natural body of water, frogs may find it! The common green frog, seen here, is similar in size to the bullfrog but displays a ridge down its back from its prominent eardrum. His favorite food is your small fish.

frogs are slightly larger but still change into their adult form within a few weeks. Larger frogs—the green frog, the leopard frog, and the bullfrog—provide amazing entertainment. I call the green frog the "banjo" frog since its call sounds like a strum on that musical instrument. The bullfrog, of course, emits the notorious "baroom" that echoes in the night. These larger frogs will not only breed in your pond, they take up permanent residence, remaining in their idyllic habitat as long as food is available. Their primary food, of course, is your fish. For that reason, I list them as predators.

Large adult frogs feast on fish fry and small fish. A friend

The Southern leopard frog is one of the larger species of frog that will consider your pet fish to be dinner.
Photo by Ron Everhart

of ours was dismayed one day to notice the splayed tail of one of her fantail goldfish jutting from the wide mouth of a bullfrog. "Do something!" she shouted to her husband. Well-trained in emergencies, our hero grabbed the frog and performed something similar to the Heimlich maneuver, thereby releasing the fish. If your small fish are special to you, or if you are purposefully breeding them, net the pond completely to pre-

vent large, predatory frogs from taking up residence. Do not deliberately introduce tadpoles into your pond. The tadpoles often sold by nurseries or bait shops are the larger tadpoles of green frogs, bullfrogs, and sometimes leopard frogs. They are predators of your pond fish.

Hatching from rounded, jelly masses laid in the pond, large frog tadpoles may take up to two years to change into their adult form. This means that in temperate ponds they must hibernate during the cold winter months. If you decide to jump-start the season and repot your aquatic plants in early spring, be prepared for the startling discovery of a mud-covered frog leaping into your face. One way to provide winter quarters for your larger frogs is to place a pot of bare soil in the bottom of your pond. If you use gravel toppings on your aquatic plant pots or if your pots are filled with root masses, a mud pot ensures your favorite frog's survival. During their winter hibernation, frog metabolism slows enough that a frog can remain buried in mud under water for a long nap.

Environmental researchers have postulated that frogs are a barometer of the health of the water environment. Such research explores the possible effect of depleting ozone layers and resulting UV radiation on the thin skin of a frog to explain

an increase in deformities and declines in populations. The effects of pollution, primarily from pesticides and herbicides, are also being studied. Preliminary results suggest that such pollution does impact frog populations. If you would encourage an amphibian population in your backyard pond, avoid chemicals.

Non-Predatory Pond Visitors

Whatever your type of pond, other critters may find it. If yours is a water garden with goldfish, these uninvited guests may be a real treat.

Toads and Tree Frogs

Even in the urban garden, toads and tree frogs appear miraculously when you put in a pond. Although both species live their adult lives within the terrestrial garden, they breed in water. You'll know they have arrived when you hear them calling to each other during the breeding season. Toads emit a high-pitched trill; the Fowler toad's trill is more pleasing to the ear, and the American toad's is more shrill. Their calling lasts only through the breeding season–early to mid-summer.

Tree frogs breed in water

but spend the rest of their lives in the garden. These are the ones with the toe-pads you occasionally find plastered to your glass doors and windows. Their mating calls are phenom-

A tree frog baby, ready to leave its pond nursery, is incredibly tiny!

enally loud for such a small creature, literally rattling the windowpanes.

If you inspect your pond after hearing the calls from the previous night, you might notice jelly strings draped among your emergent aquatic plants. Depending on the water temperature, the jelly dissolves as the eggs mature and hatch into tiny, black tadpoles within three to five days. Often they congregate in the shallow water, seeming to sunbathe on cooler days. You might notice them nibbling on the mossy algae that naturally coats the pot and pond sides. They enjoy nibbling on filamentous algae, too.

As the tadpoles begin to change into toads, they swim to

the surface to gulp air. At the same time, tiny hind legs begin to form even as their tadpole tails shorten. The metamorphosis from tadpole into toad or tree frog takes but a few weeks. You might notice the tiny toads and frogs, a stub of a tail remaining, perched on water lily leaves or on the pond edge. They are no bigger than a tiny fingernail! Leaving the pond, they take up residence in the surrounding garden, where they eat insects.

Toads are part of the food chain. While they eat insects, they are also food for other animals. Large birds may feast on tiny toads. Even within the pond, large fish may help reduce their number. Those that survive offer natural control of garden insects.

While the adult toad has dry, bumpy skin, it still requires cool and damp earth to burrow in. Commercial toad houses, nothing more than upside-down terra-cotta pots, are designed to enhance such conditions. Cultivated soil, bark mulch, and leafy foliage on the ground provide natural toad habitat.

A chemical-saturated environment endangers toad survival in the garden. Water gardeners are often cautioned to construct their ponds to avoid the possibility of surface runoff that might contain harmful chemicals and to avoid spraying chemicals near the

Toads lay eggs in long strands of jelly, compared to the round masses of frog eggs. This photo shows both the strands of eggs along with a probable parent, a toad.

Toad tadpoles are small and black. During the cooler breeding times of spring and early summer, they congregate in shallow waters to bask in the sun.

pond where airborne toxins can drift into the water. If you wish your garden to provide a healthy and safe home for the tadpoles hatched within your pond, seek natural ways to control insect pests and plant diseases. Just as you seek to balance the life within the water, so, too, try to balance the life around it, so everything can work together.

Toads hibernate during the cold winter months. Burrowing into soft soil, they tuck themselves in as their metabolisms slow for a long winter's nap. You'll know winter is over when you hear their mating calls again in the spring.

Tree frogs are other urban dwellers that will seek out your pond for breeding. Very small frogs with distinctive suction pads on each toe, these well-camouflaged creatures call to each other in spring to midsummer. The green tree frog, common in temperate zones, emits a shrill clatter as its mating call. It is an amazingly loud and robust sound for so small an animal! On the West Coast of the U.S. and across the South, barking tree frogs punctuate the night. Yet another species has been introduced in Florida, the Cuban tree frog.

All these species breed in your ponds. Since they are frogs, their jelly mass of eggs takes the form of a glob of eggs rather than the strands of eggs deposited by toads. Like toad tadpoles, the tiny hatchlings are dark colored. As they grow larger, they develop a fancy aspect to their tail—a noticeable iridescence. Changing into their adult form within a few weeks, they perch among aquatic plants or cling to plant stems above the water. With pointed noses, they barely measure an inch long! They, too, leave the water with only a stub of a tail remaining, to take up residence

Other Life Attracted to the Garden Pond

among the terrestrial garden plants. Most tree frogs are chameleonlike in their ability to change color to match the surrounding foliage. Avoiding the use of toxic chemicals in the garden ensures their survival.

Newts and Salamanders

Newts and mudpuppies are the amphibious forms of various species of salamander that may either appear in your pond voluntarily or be purchased from pet stores. Often they may visit your pond for breeding, just like the neighborhood toads. However, you may not realize they are present. They are nocturnal and very shy. The one newt encounter in my own ponds occurred when I

Newts are actually the amphibious larvae form of salamanders, comparable to the tadpole form of frogs and toads. Photo by Ron Everhart

removed a potted plant for repotting in early summer. The newt, a most slimy creature, was as surprised as I was. Supposedly good for pond-cleaning chores, newts are not fully amphibious. Like toads, parent salamanders merely breed in the pond waters, returning to terrestrial conditions. Newts remain in the water until metamorphosis. If you would harbor these interesting critters, keep a pot of bare soil within the pond depths. They appreciate the same terrestrial garden conditions as toads. Do not plan on seeing them except for brief and very occasional moments.

Snails

Many water gardening sources suggest snails as a part of your pond-stocking, even suggesting one snail per square foot of water surface. Of course, snails breed prolifically and do not even need a mate. Each snail assumes the functions of both sexes in procreation. In stocking a pond with the suggested number of snails, you soon find yourself inundated with the creatures!

Most sources differentiate among snail species as desirable or not. The tall, pointed snail known as the great pond snail is not advised since it possesses a voracious appetite for plants. In a cultivated water garden, this

can be most disfiguring. The best control is prevention. Closely check all new plants for both the snails and for gelatinous patches of their eggs on the undersides of lily leaves and on the submerged stems of aquatic plants. (The often-recommended ramshorn snail

The three most common snails found in garden ponds are the ramshorn snail, an egg-bearer (top), the great pond snail, another egg-bearer (middle), and the trapdoor snail, a live-bearer (bottom). All are intermediary hosts to parasites that prey upon your fish. Photo by Ron Everhart

lays its eggs in a circular jelly mass that is easily distinguishable from the elongated jelly mass of the great pond snail.) Use a strong hose jet to rinse all new plants. Many water gardeners also dip their new plants in a treatment tub of salt water, potassium permanganate solution (to a light pink color), or other insecticides. Never use such treatments in the pond itself, to avoid risking your other pondlife. What do you do if your pond is already infested with these snails? Manually removing them throughout the season will keep their damage under control. Then, in the autumn or in the spring, fully empty your pond for a thorough cleaning. This will rid you of these pests. Remember, however, they hibernate by burying themselves in mud. Depending on the time of year you perform a total pond cleanout, you may wish also to repot every plant, carefully hosing all soil from the plant roots before repotting in fresh soil.

Snails suggested as desirable for their algae-cleaning feeding are the tropical apple snail, the live-bearing trapdoor snail, and the egg-laying ramshorn snail. Just because these three species are recommended for water gardens does not mean they will not eat your aquatic plants. In some cases, they, too, can cause disfigurement, but their damage is usually insignificant and is outweighed by their benefits.

Even though snails are part of the pond ecology, introducing them into your pond should not be done without careful consideration. If your pond is constructed so birds can drink from it, either from the pond side or from the waterfall or stream, providing snails may not be in the best interest of

your fish. Snails are the intermediary host to parasites that infect fish and that are introduced into the pond by birds. For the best health of your fish, you may decide not to include snails at all. If you do include snails, remember to check your fish for anchor worm in the early spring and in the late fall when their immune systems are weaker and they are more susceptible to parasites.

Insects

Mosquitoes

Certain insects are attracted to water features in your garden. The most obvious, of course, are mosquitoes. Requiring water in which to lay their eggs in floating rafts that quickly hatch into aquatic larvae, mosquitoes breed in calm waters. You won't find them using your waterfall or slow-moving streams. Their control is built into your pond–your fish. Mosquito larvae, along with the tiny water flea (*Daphnia*) and other single-celled animals, provide necessary protein in the diet your fish need, especially in the spring and for young fish. In the tub garden or the fish-free pond, use *Bacillus thuringiensis*, bacteria that parasitize mos-

Mosquitoes are the most common pest to visit your pond. Without keeping fish, you might notice the whip-swimming larvae in the water.
Photo by Ron Everhart

quito larvae and kill them. These bacteria are prepared for pond introduction in the form of floating, time-release, doughnut-shaped dunks.

Midges

In the early evening you might notice what appears to be clouds of mosquitoes swarming above the surface of the pond. These are usually midges that take advantage of the water to lay eggs. While your fish may eat the midge eggs, once the larvae have hatched, they become inaccessible to both fish

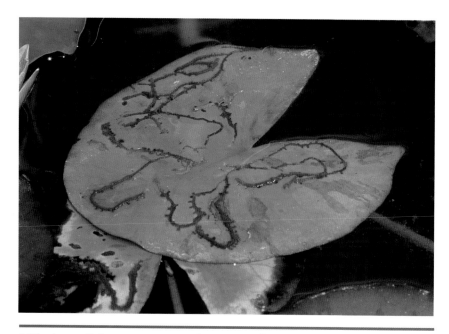

Midge larvae disfigure your aquatic plants, especially water lilies.
Photo by Ron Everhart

leaves, they lay their eggs in concentric circles on the underside of the pad. As long as the moth larvae are exposed, they can be controlled with *Bacillus thuringiensis* (*Bt*), which is commonly available in garden centers. These bacteria parasitize the intestinal tract of caterpillars and effect their death. In a pond with no fish, even mosquito larvae can be controlled with time-release floating forms of these bacteria. Some moth larvae, however, protect themselves by wrapping themselves within plant foliage and pieces of floating debris or by burrowing into the stems of the plants. Their feeding is disfiguring at the least, and is destructive. Remove affected leaves and keep floating debris from the pond's surface to aid in control. It is safe to remove all foliage from a healthy water lily; the plant will soon send up fresh growth. In severe infestations, you can remove affected plants to a separate treatment tub and use chemical remedies, rinsing the plants well before returning them to the pond. For the sake of the animal life in your pond, never use chemical pesticides within the waters.

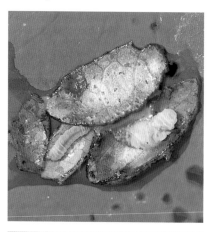

Moth larvae often conceal themselves between pieces of leaves and floating debris so they can feed unhindered upon your aquatic plants.
Photo by Ron Everhart

Moth larvae eventually make their way to the petiole of the leaf, where they begin burrowing down the stem, to pupate around the lily's rhizome. A bulge in the leaf stem indicates their presence.

and chemical controls as they burrow into epidural surfaces of plants. Control their populations by removing affected leaves.

Moths

Moths will also be drawn to your pond. Often taking advantage of holes in water lily

Aphids

Aphids are another insect pest commonly encountered in the pond. These small, sucking insects are attracted by aging and yellowing foliage. If you keep your aquatic plants pruned of dying foliage you are not likely to wage major battles with these tiny insects. However, the presence of a nearby plum or cherry tree may negate your best control efforts, since aphids winter over in these trees. Using a horticultural oil spray in the winter will prevent their summer onslaught. In spite of your efforts, they may still come. Mixing a container of vegetable oil with a splash of dishwashing detergent and spraying it on the affected plants will suffocate the pests. Remember to remove the oil film from the pond, however, as it will prevent the water from accessing ambient air for gas exchanges. Either flood the pond or use oil-absorbent paper/cloth to remove the oil once it has finished the job.

Even though the above insects are not desirable in your pond, they are a part of the natural environment in which you have created your pond. They are part of the food chain– feeding your fish, feeding the frogs and toads, feeding the birds, and feeding other lives in your backyard habitat. You don't want to decimate their population; you want only to control them for the least disfigurement of your garden creation.

Dragonflies

Dragonflies and damselflies, closely related cousins, patrol your pond and backyard in a never-ending quest for food. Feeding upon smaller insects, they are a most beneficial garden visitor. When you see them hover over the water's surface, tail dipped into the water, they are laying eggs. Their larvae are fully aquatic. The metamorphosis into adulthood is indicated by the empty shell left among your aquatic plants where they have climbed from the water, left their shell, dried their wings, and flown away. Dragonfly larvae are like the larger frog tadpoles in that

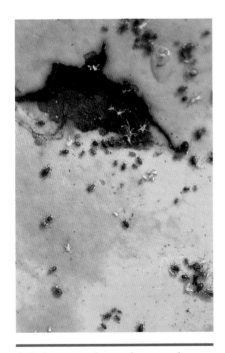

Aphids commonly attack many of your aquatic pond plants.
Photo by Ron Everhart

Damselflies are distinguished by their habit of folding their wings when at rest, as opposed to the open, at-rest wings of their cousins, the dragonflies.
Photo by Ron Everhart

Dragonflies are one of the delightful insects that visit your pond.

Surround your pond with butterfly-attractive plants.

they take two seasons to complete their transformation. They hibernate on the pond bottom or in the gravel toppings of your submersed plant pots. Cleaning the pond in autumn or spring warrants special care to preserve these larvae. What do they eat? Other small insect larvae and fish fry.

Earth-Friendly Gardening

Practice organic gardening. Lawn chemicals, whether herbicides or pesticides, can kill the life in your pond and the life attracted to it through sprays or runoff. Reassess how you view pests in your garden. Killing off all the slugs and snails, for example, bears visible and problematic repercussions within the food chain. Insects that normally would feed on them may disappear, for example. Those same insects may be beneficial insects within your garden habitat. Using organic controls ensures the Earth-friendly garden.

Plant your garden with wildlife-attractive plants. Berry-bearing shrubs, for example, provide food, cover, and nesting for birds. Consider your landscaping as a three-dimensional project—the floor of your garden, a mid-level layer that provides food, cover, and nesting, and an upper story that provides at least one higher tree for perching and nesting. Visit your local garden center and explore the world of native plants that might flourish within your garden creation even as they provide sustenance to wildlife. Consider, too, the effect of hybrids and cultivars upon the environment. Many beautiful cultivars can escape into the wild to threaten, suffocate, and eradicate native species that may be critical to the survival of the wildlife in your area.

Butterflies

The presence of butterflies in the garden lifts your spirits. Many people devote whole sections of their gardens to satisfying the needs of these special visitors. While much is written about what plants to use in attracting them, consider butterflies as "puddling" insects, requiring water like all other living creatures. Consider creating a special water feature for the butterflies.

Use a scrap piece of pond liner to hold a shallow excavation filled with soil and kept moist with a dripper or a mister. The soil can be maintained moist enough to attract and nourish butterflies.

PLANTS FOR BUTTERFLIES
The plants suggested here can attract butterflies to your water garden. Check with your county extension agent to learn

Cosmos, a delightful summer annual plant, attracts butterflies to your water feature. Why not plant it next to a "butterfly pond"?

which butterflies are indigenous in your area. Don't forget to check which plants the butterfly larvae need, too. Encouraging the butterflies to stay in your backyard can be as simple as growing a small patch of parsley. Be sure to include butterfly-attractive plants in your water garden. Pickerel weed, *Pontederia*, is a perennial blue-to-purple blooming plant that attracts butterflies. *Mentha aquatica*, water mint, hardy in zones 5–9, provides fluffy, lavender-pink blooms over a long summer season. Plant this one in soggy areas, in shallow water, or in a specially constructed bog garden where it can scramble vigorously at will. The large plant family of *Mimulus*, monkey flower, offers many annual and perennial butterfly-attractive selections, too. A relatively new tropical plant for the water garden is *Gymnocoronis*, a bushy plant with very small powder-puff white flowers that prove irresistible to monarch butterflies. Your garden pond completes the butterfly garden.

Butterfly-Attractive Plants

Remember to check with your county extension agent for the butterfly species in your area. Be sure to include both nectar-bearing flowers along with plants for the growing larvae. Plants that appreciate moist but well-drained soil are marked with a single asterisk. Plants suitable for growing in your pond or soggy soils are marked with a double asterisk. Annuals are noted with an "A" and perennials are noted with their hardiness zones. Biennial plants are designated with a "B."

Abelia chinensis, Abelia (7– 9)

Achillea millefolium, Yarrow, Milfoil (3–8)

Ageratum houstonianum, Ageratum, Flossflower (A)

Allium, Flowering onion (4–10)

Amorpha canescens, Lead plant (2–6)

Anaphalis margaritacea, Pearly everlasting (4–8)

Antennaria, Pussytoes (4–7)

Asclepias curassavica, Bloodflower (10)

Asclepias tuberosa, Butterfly weed (4–9)*

Asclepias syriaca, Common milkweed (4–9)

Aster ericoides, Heath, Many-flowered aster (5–8)

Aster × frikartii, Frikart aster (5–8)

Aster lateriflorus, Calico aster (4–8)

Aurinia saxatilis, Basket of gold (4–8)

Barbarea vulgaris, St. Barbara's herb (4–9)

Bougainvillea (9–11)

Buddleia alternifolia, Fountain butterfly bush (6–9)

Buddleia davidii, Orange-eye butterfly bush, Summer lilac (6–9)

Camassia scilloides, Wild hyacinth (3–10)

Ceanothus americanus, New Jersey tea (4–8)*

Ceanothus thyrsiflorus, Wild lilac, Blueblossom (8–10)

Centaurea, Knapweed, Bachelor's button, Cornflower (A)

Centranthus ruber, Red valerian (5–8)

Cephalanthus occidentalis, Buttonbush (5–10)**

Cercis canadensis, Redbud (5–9)

Chrysanthemum vulgare, Ox-eye daisy (3–8)*

Chrysanthemum maximum, Shasta daisy (5–8)

Cleome hasslerana, Spider flower (A)

Clethra alnifolia, Summersweet, Sweet pepperbush (3–9)*

Cordia boisseri, Anacahuita (10–11)

Coreopsis verticillata, Thread-leaved coreopsis (4–9)

Coreopsis lanceolata, Lance-leaved coreopsis (4–9)

Coreopsis grandiflora, Coreopsis, tickseed(4–9)

Cosmos bipinnatus, Cosmos (A)

Dalea purpurea, Purple prairie clover (9–11)

Dianthus barbatus, Sweet William (B; 3–8)

Dianthus armeria, Deptford pink (4–8)

Dichelostemma pulchellum, Blue-dick (6–10)

Echinacea purpurea, Purple coneflower (3–9)

Echinacea angustifolia, Purple coneflower (4–9)

Erigeron, Fleabane (5–8)

Erythrina herbacea, Coral bean (8–10)

Escallonia spp., Cultivars (8–9)

Eupatorium rugosum, White snakeroot (4–9)*

Eupatorium fistulosum, Trumpetweed (3–8)*

Eupatorium maculatum, Smoke weed (3–7)*

Eupatorium coelestinum, Hardy ageratum, Mistflower (3–7)

Euphorbia marginata, Snow-on-the-mountain (A)

Filipendula purpurea, Queen of the meadow, Japanese meadowsweet (4–9)

Fragaria virginiana, Wild strawberry (5–9)

Gaillardia pulchella, Indian blanket (A)

Gazania, Teasure flower (8–10)

Geranium, Cranesbill, Wild geranium (4–8)

Gomphrena globosa, Globe amaranth (A)

Grindelia, Gumweed (7–9)

Gymnocoronis (10–11)**

Helenium autumnale, Sneezeweed (4–8)

Helianthus angustifolia, Swamp sunflower (6–9)*

Heliopsis helianthoides, Ox-eye (4–9)*

Heliotropium arborescens, Heliotrope (A)

Hemerocallis spp., Daylily (3–10)*

Hesperis matronalis, Sweet rocket (4–9)

Heterotheca villosa, Hairy golden aster (4–10)

Isatis tinctoria, Dyer's wood (B; 4–8)

Lantana (A)

Lathyrus latifolius, Everlasting pea (5–9)

Lavandula dentata, French lavender, Fringed lavender (8–9)

Lavandula angustifolia, Lavender (5–8)

Ledum groenlandicum, Labrador tea (2–6)*

Liatris, Gayfeather, Blazing star (3–9)

Ligustrum, Privet (3–10)

Limonium latifolium, Sea lavender/Statice (4–9)

Lobelia cardinalis, Cardinal flower (3–9)

Lobelia erinus, Edging lobelia (A)

Lonicera japonica, Japanese honeysuckle (4–10)

Lupinus perennis, Wild lupine (4–9)

Mentha spp., Mint (3–9)

Mikania scandens, Climbing hempweed (10–11)

Mirabilis jalapa, Four-o'clock (A)

Monarda fistulosa, Wild bergamot (3–9)

Monarda didyma, Bee balm/Oswego tea (4–9)

Myosotis scorpioides (palustris) Water forget-me-not (5–9)**

Nepeta cataria, Catnip (3–7)

Nicotiana alata, Flowering tobacco (A)

Oenothera, Evening primrose (3–8)

Opuntia compressa, Prickly pear (6–8)

Petunia × hybrida (A)

Philadelphus coronarius, Mock orange (5–8)

Physocarpus monogynus, Mountain ninebark (5–8)

Plumbago auriculata, Cape leadwort (9–10)

Potentilla fruticosa, Shrubby cinquefoil (3–7)

Prunella grandiflora, Selfheal (5–8)

Ratibida columnifera, Prairie coneflower (3–10)

Rhododendron pericylmenoides (R. nudiflorum), Pinxter flower, Pink azalea (4–9)

Rhus aromatica, Fragrant sumac (4–9)

Rhus typhina, Staghorn sumac (3–8)

Rhus glabra, Smooth sumac (2–9)

Rosmarinus officinalis, Rosemary (8–10)

Rubus spp., Blackberry, Raspberry (5–9)

Rudbeckia laciniata, Green-headed coneflower (3–9)

Rudbeckia fulgida, Black-eyed Susan (4–9)

Rudbeckia hirta, Gloriosa daisy (3–7)

Ruellia, Wild petunia (10–11)

Salvia spp., Sage (5–10)

Scabiosa caucasica, Scabiosa (4–9)

Schinus terebinthifolius (9–10)

Solidago, Goldenrod (5–8)

Sophora arizonica (9–11)

Symphytum officinale, Comfrey (3–9)

Syringa vulgaris, Lilac (4–8)

Tagetes Hero Series, French marigold (A)

Thymus spp., Thyme (4–10)

Vaccinium corymbosum, Highbush blueberry (3–7)

Verbena hastata, Blue vervain (4–7)

Verbena candensis, Rose vervain (4–7)

Verbena × hybrida (A)

Veronia noveboracensis, Ironweed (5–9)

Zinnia (A)

Converting to Metric

To Convert	Multiply by	To Obtain
inches	2.54	centimeters
inches	25.4	millimeters
feet	30	centimeters
pounds	0.45	kilograms
U.S. gallons	3.8	liters

Fahrenheit to Celsius: Subtract 32, multiply by 5, divide by 9.

Index

W

water, pond, 75-85
  algae control in, 85-87
  ammonia in, 79-80
  changing of, 83-84
  chloramine in, 75-76
  chlorine in, 75-76
  dissolved oxygen in, 82-83
  hydrogen sulfide in, 84-85
  nitrate in, 81-82
  nitrite in, 80-81
  nitrogen cycle in, 78-79
  pH of, 76-78
  temperature of, 84
  testing of, 64, 69, 72, 83
  waterfall/stream, installation of, 36-38
water-quality factors affecting fish
  ammonia in water, 103-104
  chloramine in water, 103
  chlorine in water, 103
  copper and simazine in water, 105-106
  dissolved oxygen in water, 104-105
  hydrogen sulfide in water, 105
  nitrate in water, 104
  nitrite in water, 104
  toxic runoffs, 105
  water temperature, 102-103
worms, 127